"If your business is about you and you're building a personal brand, then it's essential that you look for ways to stand out against the competition by establishing authority in your field."

Stephanie Chandler
Forbes Contributor

"Few people have the ability to write and deliver a message like David."

Les Brown
Recognized as the World's #1 Speaker

"David Fagan has a Ph.D. from the University of Experience. He's faced daunting challenges, and through creativity and hard work, reinvented himself as an icon in his arena. This book shares his insights, strategies, and tactics. If you're willing to do the work, these ideas will pay off richly.

Mark Sanborn
President, Sanborn & Associates, Inc.
New York Times Bestselling Author of *The Fred Factor*

"David is being too humble. His new book, *Cracking the Icon Code*, doesn't just crack it… it SHATTERS it!

Steven Memel
Performance Coach, as seen on MTV's *Made*

"David has always had a way of attracting big-time clients and even bigger opportunities. I've personally witnessed his rise to become an Icon himself and how he shares his secrets in this book. It takes the formula that was at one time only in his head as pure instinct and now delivers it step by step to the rest of us. It is my belief that if you can harness only half of this book you will still be twice as successful!"

W. Roger Salam
Author, Speaker, and Founder of *The Winners Circle*

Cracking the
Icon Code

Cracking the Icon Code

**Learn How to Become an
Icon in Your Industry through
Image, Expertise, and Advice**

———

David T. Fagan

Beverly Hills, California

Cracking the Icon Code: Learn How to Become an Icon in Your Industry through Image, Expertise, and Advice, 2nd Edition

Copyright © 2015 by David T. Fagan
www.IconCoach.com
david@davidtfagan.com

Published by Silver Torch Publishing
www.SilverTorchPublishing.com

Library of Congress Control Number 2015913709
ISBN 978-1-942707-16-5

Cover and back design by Carli Smith.

Printed in the United States of America.

Table of Contents

Special Thanks

To my mentors Jay Conrad Levinson "The Father of Guerrilla Marketing", Diana von Welanetz Wentworth, Steve Jennings, Ted Wentworth, Steven Memel, John Maxwell, Dan Kennedy, Roger Salam, Dan Clark, and John Assaraf.

To the Staff of Silver Torch Publishing for all that you do.

And a special thanks to Kaitlin, the best publicist I have ever had. You have given me iconic opportunities. Don't ever stop being you.

Introduction

There are no silver bullets in business. Nothing works every time for every person in every place. The idea is to learn the best business practices that you can play day in and day out through wisdom. This is playing the odds.

The best and most successful decision makers know how to gain knowledge and recognize what truth has the greatest value in every situation.

This book is filled with best practices as well as laws of the universe that, once understood and implemented, will drastically improve your chances at success. In many ways this book actually gives you an unfair advantage over all your competition. You will see exactly what I mean, chapter by chapter.

Cracking the Icon Code is an entirely different decision making matrix. It's an approach and a way of understanding the world around you. It's working with the way people already think. Whether you agree with the way most people are or not isn't the issue at hand.

Some people only exercise the strategy of hoping their talent will be discovered someday. Being discovered isn't just for actors and musicians, but you can't just wish for it. You have to work for it. The good news is that there is, in fact, a formula for launching and maintaining a business icon status in your industry.

The teachings in this book will show you how to authentically profit from publicity, positioning, and posturing in the market place. Discover the power of being a celebrity expert.

Part I

The Icon Approach

"Be so good
they can't
ignore you."

~ Steve Martin

Chapter 1

ICE in Your Veins

You must first ask yourself these three questions:

1. Would I make more money if I had more **I**nfluence?
2. Would I make more money if I had more **C**redibility?
3. Would I make more money if I had more **E**xposure?

If you answered yes to any of these questions, you need to read every word in this book. This is my ICE acronym. It's changing lives and making people lots of money. There is nothing like having even a little ice in your veins. It's at the core of an Icon and paramount for people in the advice business—those who make money off the advice they give.

If you are in the advice business, then you are selling yourself as much as anything else. That's right. People are buying you more than any product or service you sell.

Speakers, coaches, consultants, and "how to" authors are all in the advice business. So are attorneys, dentists, doctors, contractors, accountants, bankers, real estate agents, network marketers, and veterinarians. These industries cover hundreds of various job titles, and they all make money off the advice they give. Let me tell you a story to illustrate this point.

There was once a power plant humming along, providing power to the nearby town. One morning, as the foreman and his crews went throughout the plant with work as usual, they heard a loud pop. Suddenly, there was no power to the nearby town.

5

DO YOU INFLUENCE THE AFFLUENT?

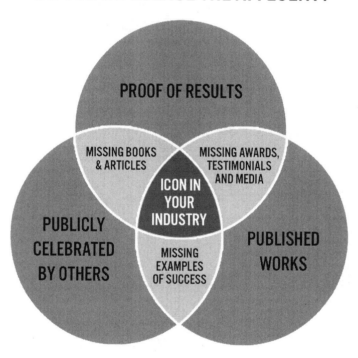

Workers scrambled into action, going through the standard checklists to see what went wrong. The situation was unsafe, scary, and potentially volatile for the workers and the townspeople.

One person mentioned to the foreman that they may want to call in a specialist. He knew of someone whose reputation was stellar. After all, time was of the essence, and they needed whatever help they could get as soon as possible.

The foreman reluctantly agreed, the secretary made the call, and the specialist rushed over. After a series of questions posed from the specialist to the foreman, the specialist knew exactly where he wanted to go first.

The whole crew followed the legendary specialist around the plant for long minutes as he asked more questions and investigated the situation. After less than ten minutes, the specialist walked straight over to a big gray box, took out a black marker, and put an "X" on the box.

He pointed with confidence. "You fix this, and everything will work again."

The crew immediately went to work, and soon the problem was solved. The switch was flipped, and the power started humming right along. The town was powered, and the crew was relieved. Everyone was happy and thankful, and the specialist went home.

Several days later, the secretary got a bill in the mail. It was for $10,000! The secretary was astonished. After all, it took her almost half a year to make that kind of money. She quickly went to the foreman and showed him the bill. The foreman was shocked and quickly handed the bill back to her. "You send that back and ask for an itemized breakdown of costs," he said.

The secretary and foreman got a new, itemized invoice a week later that read:

Dear Foreman,

Black X: $1

Knowing where to put that Black X: $9,999

Sincerely,
The Specialist

Are you a specialist? Does your reputation precede you? Do you get paid what you are worth for knowing where to put that black X? There is a lot that can be learned from this story, and I tell it often.

So if *you* are the real product, then it's your Icon status that matters the most. Some may call it being a trusted advisor, a trusted authority, or even an expert authority, but none of those will separate you from the competition the way being an Icon in your industry can. However, even being an Icon means very little if you don't know how to monetize your knowledge and experiences.

The specialist in the previous story was an Icon because his reputation preceded him. He was a legend to those crewmen. He asked the right questions, gave the right answer, and charged accordingly. It's worth noting that people often must already know you and see you as a solution before the problem ever presents itself.

That's why this book will cover four main topics:

1. The Icon Approach
2. Your Icon Solar System
3. Monetizing Your Icon Status
4. Your Icon Evolution

In addition, you will find a healthy amount of information on mindset and mentality in the fast chapters ahead. The first step in taking Icon-worthy action is to continually internalize the right thoughts and feelings.

Chapter 2

Making Your Presence Felt

When I was young, I became very aware of the limitations of my "first impressions". Although the gray hair is coming in nicely now, I have always looked very young for my age. So young that people just wouldn't take me seriously. For a driven, determined person to not be taken seriously is a fate worse than death.

I have always been very independent. I was in a hurry to walk, talk, to ride a bike, and especially to drive. After all, this is how things get done and life gets experienced. I also learned that working and making money were the very keys to the existence of my greater independence.

As a kid, I did yard work. At 13 I had a paper route, at 14 I was a housekeeper for Best Western Hotel during the summer, at 15 I worked as a grounds keeper at a care center and stocked shelves at Newberry's, and at 16 and 17 I delivered furniture.

Although I love physically hard work, I started to make some observations. Everywhere I worked there was someone inside an office managing, leading, and advising. It appeared to me that they physically worked less, and yet they made more money. Although I didn't care about the physical work, I did care about making more money! Money equaled independence and self-reliance.

But it was even more than money. It was having opportunities, having friends, and especially getting the attention of girls. (I know, it's all pretty embarrassing.) It was learning to want the right things (which we should call step one) and learning how to get what I wanted (we will call this step two). Step one is twice as important as step two.

So now I knew what I wanted...at least for the time being. I wanted and needed to be taken seriously and given a chance to make good money leading and advising. There were just two major problems staring me in the face. One, I looked very young; and two...I hated school.

Who was going to listen to a young, uneducated guy who looked like a kid?! How was I going to influence, persuade, and inspire people? And so the discovery was realized, and the journey began. At first it was mostly trial and error. But over time, I was able to hammer out an exact formula for success that I've been able to apply again and again.

I have had my own radio show, written and published books and magazines, spoken to thousands of people and hundreds of audiences nationally and internationally, shared the stage with Mark Victor Hansen, Jay Conrad Levinson, Diana Wentworth, Dan Kennedy, John Assaraf, Harry Dent, Michael Gerber, former Secretary of Defense Dr. Bob Gates, owned as many as 26 properties at once, am the former CEO of Guerrilla Marketing, and I have made good money. My clients have been seen on every major media outlet and on all the major talk shows. Just in the last year, I have been featured on *Fox and Friends, Your World with Neil Cavuto, The Today Show, The Five, The Doctors Show,* and have been in *Forbes, MSN, Yahoo Parenting,* the *Washington Post,* and interviewed by the *Financial Times* and the *Daily Mail,* both out of London.

And yet...I started but never finished high school; I only have a GED. I started but never finished college; I have maybe 40 credits. I don't have wealthy parents. I don't have any more time than any of you do; if anything I have less time with eight children, several businesses, a physically active lifestyle, and involvement in church keeping me pretty busy.

So how do I do it? I do it through the art of making my presence felt. I do it by being heard by the right people, by being seen doing the best things, and by getting the results I most desire. I have been personally perfecting this art for more than 20 years and do it by drawing on thousands of years of wisdom. This is my life's work.

Making your presence felt is about the look and energy that you are communicating. Sometimes making your presence felt means doing something better than everyone else. It could also mean shining bright or even just looking better than what is around you.

On the road to being a master of this art, there are a few things you need to know.

> *M*aking your presence felt is about the look and energy that you are communicating.

Your words, and ultimately your message, should be wrapped in something personal, unique, intriguing, fascinating, fun, or different.

To deliver a message with no wrapping is a waste of words! Remember, it's not always what you say, but rather how you say it. I will even go a few steps further and say it is also how you deliver that message that matters most.

The wrapping or delivery devices that can be used are very diverse. The art is to know how each works, why you would use one over another, where they might have the most impact, and when to use that particular one.

A true master will be able to know and see all this so they can apply a combination of them almost subconsciously as they simply live in a day-to-day routine.

You must start seeing everything you do as a signal, and ultimately a message you are sending. Whether it is intended or unintended, people read into these things. This actually works to your benefit if you can master the art of making your presence felt.

For example, I recently pitched the media saying that I refused to pay for my kids' college education and that college was a waste of time and money for most people. I am a big believer in customizing your education. In the past I believe it might have been safer or even more stable to go to college and then work for some big organization. You could put in your time, make decent money, and enjoy the benefits that come from a corporate lifestyle.

A lot has changed in the last decade. I believe that a lot of young people would be better off if they got to pursue a more customized education starting as early as age 12. They would be better off learning various trades, different types of software, and other real world types of job duties.

I can actually prove that many college kids are just wasting time and their parent's money by going to a college or university only to return home to live with their folks again.

To privately believe this is one thing, but I went one step further and put it out to the world. Of course, this statement wrapped my beliefs in something controversial and shocking. Just days after, I was on *Fox & Friends* in the morning discussing my beliefs about teaching people to become self-reliant through customizing their education. I taught how I will not just pay for my kid's college education and that they each are being raised to know that.

This is an example of how I took a somewhat average, almost invisible belief and turned it into something invincible that the world had to face me on.

Some may be tempted to call these devices manipulation, and that may be a fair assessment. I call this the purest form of communication. More importantly, weigh this out in your mind. Is TV good or bad? Is the Internet good or bad? Both should be met with the same answer of, "Well, that depends." The truth is, there is no right or wrong with the technology; rather its value lies in how it is used. The same applies to communication, negotiation, and even that dirty word—sales.

As a Star Wars fan, I can also relate it to "the Force". The ability to be a master Jedi is not inherently bad, but it can be used for good or evil. The information I am about to share could be used for the dark side and ultimately dark purposes. However, I choose to believe, like so many other tools and technology, the good will outweigh the bad. Here are some ways to determine if your uses are pure or corrupt.

Do you believe in your cause?

Will getting what you want benefit the ones giving, serving, and sharing with you?

If you are selling something, will those buying truly benefit?

Can you and will you fulfill on your promises?

Will you be honest in the process of wrapping your messages through different delivery devices?

If you are answering "No" or even have a hard time answering at all, then you may be trying to truly manipulate in an unfair, dirty way. If you are answering "Yes" then you are my audience.

It can take months, and even years, to master these methods, but I can promise and prove to you that once you are a master of making your presence felt there is nothing you cannot accomplish. In all reality, you will be invincible.

You may be thinking that I am asking you to compete in a never-ending beauty contest or to be a showoff, but that isn't the case at all. Of course, many times while you are in the pursuit of improving, people will think you are trying to be better than them when most of the time you should just be trying to be better, period.

There are times on a team, as a part of an organization, or even a congregation that we are not trying to really make our presence felt over anything or anyone else. In these moments we are just a part of something bigger and more than ourselves. In these moments we should blend in and play our role, our part, or position. This again is the exception to the rule.

"THERE IS AN ART TO MAKING YOUR PRESENCE FELT. TO INTRIGUE, TO FASCINATE AND ULTIMATELY TO STAND OUT IS KEY TO BEING REMEMBERED. THIS COMES FUNDAMENTALLY FIRST IN CRACKING THE ICON CODE."

~ *DAVID T. FAGAN*

www.ICONBOOTCAMP.com

But even then it's your job to help make the body that you are a part of stand out and make its presence felt. You can be a leader as the ultimate follower. When people look for answers and solutions, the inspiration will come that you are the one they need in their cause, movement, team, or business because you made your presence felt.

That being said, we have to be honest with the world we live in. We do need to compete. You will see a lot of people claiming we should all hold hands and sing kumbaya. Although I am not entirely against that, I more firmly believe that a lot of good comes to the world through competition.

Lions roar, bears growl, rattle snakes rattle, dogs bark, peacocks fan out their feathers, and apes puff out their chests. In their world, and even sometimes in our world, this is them making their presence felt. They get noticed. They get somewhat experienced. You are thinking about them in these instances and what they may or may not do. They have your attention.

Where is your roar? Where is your growl?

Chapter 3

The Humility Myth

After doing sales and marketing for twenty years and being a business owner for fifteen of those, I have been able to discover some patterns that have led me to some contrarian core beliefs. Many good people believe that humility is rewarded...even in their business.

This is the belief that says if you just work hard enough, eventually someone will recognize you, appreciate you, and even pay you good money. This is what I call the Humility Myth. Once again, good knowledge applied wrong from people acting unwisely.

There is also a belief that says sharing your successes is wrong, counterproductive, and just prideful. This is another facet of the Humility Myth!

The interesting thing is that the people who have bought into this myth are generally the same people who regularly admit to me that, although they are good at what they do, they are terrible marketers and poor salespeople.

There really is an art of being heard, being seen, and getting results. It's one of the core principles in my book *From Invisible to Invincible*. What so many misunderstand is that promoting yourself isn't about you directly saying how great you are; rather it's about you indirectly having others tell the world how great you are.

Testimonials, awards, endorsements, media mentions, and features are just a few ways to do this. You have to be able to capture and document your success so it can be shared with the world strategically.

Video strategies and other visual aids can be huge in getting people's attention, teaching your ideal prospects, and being unforgettable. Here are just a few visual strategies I create and use.

1. Timeline Images—Create images that show your biggest milestones over the course of a certain period of time.
2. Top Ten Lists—Create lists of the Top Ten reasons that people listen to you or work with you.
3. Infographics—Create metaphors or analogies that combine images, words, and numbers to make something that's complicated more simple.
4. Workflow Charts—Create step-by-step processes of how you work with people or help people make decisions and get things done.
5. Memes—Create posters that combine words with images that, when put together, evoke a strong emotional trigger.

Say thank you when people compliment you. Please "give" with no agenda from time to time, and have some unadvertised bonuses as well. Be charitable, and serve in secret occasionally.

BUT, BUT, BUT don't be afraid to apply and compete for business. Be prepared with social proof to share with prospects why they should hire you, promote you, or even work with you.

Some may say that they get business by being humble, but I would change that to point out that they get business despite being humble. If you really want to be humble, then be teachable right now and work to understand what I am saying to you. You're not bragging in business; you are applying for a job!

Yes, you need strategy. Yes, you need other people and organizations to do most of the bragging. Yes, you need social proof in general to share all the time.

This is even truer for speakers, authors, and experts. Some of the best entrepreneurs you know are the ones who get the most exposure being heard and being seen doing all the right things.

Donald Trump, Mark Cuban, Simon Cowell, and Richard Branson are not necessarily the most knowledgeable; rather, they are the most known due to good marketing and publicity. These men are not known for being humble, although you might be shocked to know how much they actually give away.

Stop easing your conscience and rationalizing your fear of self-promotion because you believe you are living some higher law of humility. It's a falsehood that is unnecessary. This is just the Humility Myth.

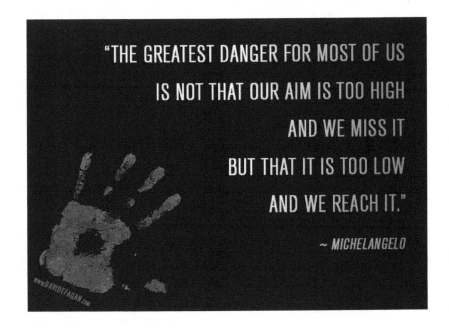

"THE GREATEST DANGER FOR MOST OF US IS NOT THAT OUR AIM IS TOO HIGH AND WE MISS IT BUT THAT IT IS TOO LOW AND WE REACH IT."

~ MICHELANGELO

Chapter 4

Tom Hanks
Taught Me to Sell

You may not know this, but Tom Hanks doesn't audition. Of course, he still gets plenty of roles in movies, and yet he never really auditions anymore. He hasn't for close to two decades is my guess!

You see, his awards, his star power, his ticket sales, and his overall body of work speak for themselves. You know what you get when you hire Tom. There really isn't a need to ask him a whole lot of questions or have him read lines to you. Every director and studio know that they would be lucky to have him.

All you really have to do is decide if you want him, then figure out if you can afford him, and ultimately see if he wants to work with you.

The truth is, he never really tries to sell anyone…and neither do I. Instead, I have worked hard to create a body of work that speaks for itself. I work even harder to make sure that I continue to create high quality and very valuable results for my clients.

So many people want the "pitch" and want me to persuade them, convince them, or even sell them. I know many times people are brought to me or referred to me with the hopes that I might sell them. Of course that's not what I do. I don't listen for objections and then craft some perfectly worded comeback so that I might overcome those objections. That's just not me.

The truth is that I don't even want to talk to people until they have seen some of my websites, they have watched the media reel of me on national TV shows, played some of my many testimonials, or read part of one or more of my books. These forms of social proof do all the selling I will ever need.

If, after hearing me speak to a group or experiencing some of my social proof, I answer some questions or even write a custom proposal, that's about it. I don't really audition. That might sound arrogant, but it's the most efficient way to run a business **IF** you have the body of work to back you up.

If they have watched me on *Your World* with Neil Cavuto, the *Today Show*, the *Five, Fox and Friends*, read my book, heard me speak, watched my testimonials, seen the finished product of happy clients, and reviewed the awards I have won, what else could I possibly say to try to convince them of my effectiveness? Not much.

You could try to go out and learn more about how to be a great salesperson, or you could go out and build the social proof you need to be a celebrity expert or an Icon in your industry. It's up to you, but people like Tom Hanks, Al Pacino, Jim Carey, Meryl Streep, Jennifer Lawrence, and Julianne Moore don't audition. You just know what you are going to get when you hire them, and I believe it's the same with me.

Want it to be the same with you? Do you have a body of work that speaks for itself?

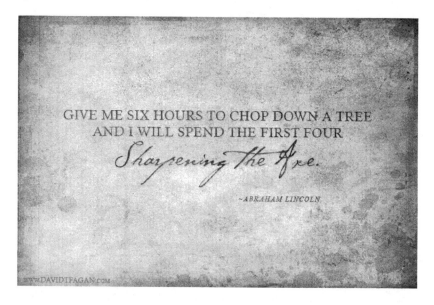

GIVE ME SIX HOURS TO CHOP DOWN A TREE
AND I WILL SPEND THE FIRST FOUR
Sharpening the Axe.

~*ABRAHAM LINCOLN*

WWW.DAVIDTPAGAN.COM

The greatest thing you could do in your business is to stop selling and to start building social proof that sells for you. It's how Tom taught me to sell.

Chapter 5

The Subtle Art of Bragging

There really is an art to bragging…and there are only a few times it's likely to be forgiven. One of those times is when you are applying for a job. This includes most marketing and advertising. Here are several ways to showcase your success, and I'll even give you some examples of my own…if you don't mind.

The first one is what I call "Top Ten Reasons Why People Listen to (fill in the blank)." You can also change this to a different number. There was a point in my career six years ago when I struggled to find five reasons. Whatever the number is, just make sure they are good and compelling pieces of social proof.

You can also change it from "Why People Listen to Me" to "Why People Hire Me" or even "Why People Buy From Me." The bottom line is that it is all about why people engage you and take action based on your involvement.

When writing out the bullets, it's best, whenever possible, to start with an action word and to use as many different action words as possible. These Top Ten lists can be on a banner, vertical screen, mailer, social media poster, or in an email. Below are examples that can be used in your marketing and custom proposals. (Always start with action words and phrases that have emotional triggers of results.)

1. Created new revenue streams at…
2. Developed new programs resulting in…
3. Built out marketing channels that…

4. Won the award for...
5. Completed courses in...
6. Achieved excellence by...
7. Earned hundreds of testimonials for...
8. Seen on these TV shows...
9. Featured in these media outlets...
10. Increased my client's revenue from...
11. Authored the book(s)...
12. Represented celebrity clients...
13. Saved clients...
14. Raised venture capital in the amount of...
15. Spoke to audiences of...
16. Shared the stage with...
17. Hosted...
18. Published in...
19. Overcame...
20. Turned around...

These are examples of how your points might start. These points could be used in ads, emails, websites, social media, and even in talking points. Numbers can be as important as starting with action words. Any way that you can show results reached in your bullets is a really smart thing to do. Be careful with numbers that are going to be more officially advertised. There can be FCC concerns, guidelines, and other issues depending on your industry.

(When reviewing resumes for interns, employees, or contractors I also look for these same examples of results-oriented success starting with action words.)

Keeping track of your accomplishments, figuring out the best way to word them, and displaying them at the right time in the right way and in the right places are just more ways to position yourself as an Icon in your industry.

Reasons and points of success are best featured when they are social proof or are coming from 3rd party sources. Degrees, media, published works, testimonials, and endorsements are great. Just ask yourself if you want to talk about yourself when you can share how others are celebrating you.

That is probably the biggest misunderstanding in cracking the icon code. People think I am asking them to just randomly go around talking about themselves, shamelessly self-promoting their business. Although there is a kernel of truth to that, the much larger truth to cracking the icon code is about strategically sharing how others love you, appreciate you, reward you, feature you, and ultimately celebrate you.

Either way, remember, you aren't bragging; you are applying for a job, and there is a difference.

SELF-CONFIDENCE
IS THE FIRST REQUISITE TO GREAT UNDERTAKINGS.
~SAMUEL JOHNSON

Chapter 6

The Unfair Icon Advantage

Disclaimer: If you do NOT like to win, do NOT believe you have the best solution in the marketplace, or do NOT want to make more money, then this next part isn't for you.

If you're still with me up to this point, you're an adult with thick skin. If this isn't you, then you need to stop reading right now because I am about to hurt your feelings. Call it tough love.

Let me give you a hypothetical situation: It's me versus you in a contest of trying to get someone to do something—anything; it really doesn't matter what it is.

For instance, we could both offer the exact same product for $1,000...and they would buy mine, not yours.

We could both offer the exact same service for $1,000...and they would buy from me, not you. I bet I could even charge twice as much as you, and they would still choose to buy from me rather than you.

Right now, you might be doing what most people do, which is to make up excuses or look for exceptions. Don't do that. Do you want to make more money and help more people? Then think about what I am telling you. You might know more than I do in a particular area; you might be more educated, or you might even have more money. But it doesn't really matter, and do you want to know why?

Because I have more social proof than you do. I have more testimonials and endorsements than you. I've probably won more awards than you, or at least more relevant awards. I've written more books than you. I've been published more than you. I have more connections than you. The truth is, you might be better. Your products and services might be better than mine, but I will win almost every time. It's unfair, isn't it?

That's right, I have an unfair advantage over my competition, and you can too.

The key is to have marketing collateral and sales tools that separate and elevate you and your company. A potential buyer is always choosing between you and something else, even if it's doing nothing at all. It's true; you are competing with the status quo, where the Prospect does nothing. You better have a really good answer when someone asks, "Why you?" or "Why you instead of (blank)?"

I love it when people ask this question of me. I take people through a funnel, daring them to ask me those questions; I can't wait! When you have good marketing collateral and social proof, you have confidence and communicate from a position of strength. When you don't, you are reluctant, hesitant, and unprepared.

I don't have to put any of my potential competitors down, and I don't. Rather, I can just show them all my social proof. I show them my YouTube channel bulging with testimonials, endorsements, case studies, and examples. I show them my portfolio showcasing the quality of my work. I put them in touch with highly successful people who love me and my work—my fans. And the list goes on.

- What do you do?
- What do you have to share?
- Is it easy to search, view, and review? If not, you might be losing in an unfair way.

If you implement what I'm about to share with you in this book, you are pages away from having an unfair advantage over your competition.

All right, here comes some more truth telling. (It's my specialty.) There will be no political correctness, and some of my close friends will disagree with what I am about to say. The "Law of Abundance" is somewhat broken—or at least, it can break you if not counter balanced correctly.

Before everyone turns hostile and starts the attack, let me explain.

Yes, there is enough out there for everyone. Yes, you can get a lot from cooperating. Yes, being friendly and professional is a must when it comes to every aspect of your business.

But somehow this common sense and decent approach to business has gone too far. You absolutely can and should:

1. Tell people how you are different.
2. Tell people what makes you great.
3. Compete to win more business.

And yes, this might just mean that if you are winning the business, then someone else is losing it. Yes, losing! And guess what? That's okay! This is a free, capitalist market. Find out what people want, and give it to them. We should all learn from our losses and become better organizations.

There is a time for cooperation and creating synergy. Just don't blur the lines and lose track of who your competitors are.

- Coke isn't in a mastermind group with Pepsi.
- McDonald's doesn't share a booth at a convention with Burger King.
- Apple doesn't send out emails for Microsoft.

The Law of the War Chest

I believe in friendly competition. I believe in personally complimenting people on their success. But I also believe in the Law of the War Chest, which states that people only have so much money in their war chest to fight the battle of day-to-day business building and life in general.

Thanks to the banks, credit lines, and the economy, that war chest has shrunk significantly. You are competing for a hard-fought treasure that is now locked up and vigilantly protected.

People will sometimes be forced to decide how they are going to spend their money, and sometimes they will not be able to do it all. There just won't be enough in the war chest.

The key to balancing cooperation and competition is focusing on others that are truly complementary. Who knows who you want to know? Who reinforces what you do and sell? Those are the people you want to collaborate and build relationships with.

You will want to create a Golden Rolodex. You need to wow influential people who have a strong following. Keep their contact info handy and review your top fifty to one hundred people weekly. I like to keep the best ones on a highly visible whiteboard in my office. Break these people up into categories. Focus on the ones who have their own radio shows, TV shows, or large email databases. Don't forget those people who have high traffic to their websites, thousands of Facebook friends, Twitter followers, and LinkedIn connections. Do whatever you can to add value to their lives. This one approach has helped positively promote and control the destiny and profitability of my business more than anything else.

Be intentional as you build your professional web of contacts. This means that your circle might be small, but it will be strong and effective in launching you into greater success. Cooperate less, Compete more, and focus on the Complementary. It's that simple. Just practice the 3 C's.

It really is okay to be against an idea, product, or service, regardless of the politically correct environment we live in today. In reality, you will go farther and attract deeper connections by causing a little controversy. I would hope this goes without saying, but I'm only asking you to stand up for what you believe. I'm NOT asking you to be mean or randomly belligerent just to get a little attention.

Here is what I am saying:

1. Talk about ideas, products, and services that don't work and why. If you are all about health and fitness like Jillian Michaels of *The Biggest Loser,* it's okay to be harsh and relatively extreme about poor lifestyle habits. Be bold. If you are about conservatism and the Republican Party like Rush Limbaugh, it's okay to attack the ideas of the Left. If you are passionate about music and art like Lady Gaga, it's okay to fight the status quo and be edgy and out there. In fact, for these people, it's more than okay; it's profitably preferred! Sometimes it's all right to be a little polarizing. The people who are your target market and fans will only gravitate closer to you. The ones you'll upset are the people who were never really your followers or clients in the first place.

2. Make bold statements to the media. Again, first you actually need to believe in your bold statements. Sharing them with the media is a great way to get free PR. Being an Icon is not for the faint of heart. Put yourself out there. Harry Dent wrote about the Roaring 2000s and a DOW Jones that would hit 20,000+ once upon a time. He believed it, and he shared the belief. Those bold predictions gave him tremendous attention. A lot of Harry's predictions have come to pass, and his Dent Method is followed in great numbers. Trump has made a brand and a presidential bid out of being bold in the media. We can all learn from this.

3. Do NOT attack people. Causing controversy goes wrong when people make it personal by attacking others. Although I can point out several profitable personal attacks—Letterman vs. Palin, Paula vs. Simon, and Yankee fans vs. Red Sox fans— typically this is risky business. Just be careful. Make sure your beliefs and integrity are in line with how you share your

feelings.

4. Use specific examples. Utilize recent newsworthy stories and events that will support your bold beliefs. Anything that can prove your cause and movement is great to leverage. I'm still not sure how to feel about how every unusual weather story gets tied to Global Warming, but it must be working. If you are against texting and driving (Who isn't? Yet who hasn't at some point?), then all the car-accident related reports are helpful, aren't they?

If you want yourself or your company to be an Icon in your industry, you need to speak up and be naturally different. You'll bond with those who agree and distance those who never mattered in the first place. If you are alienating clients and friends, then maybe you need to look at what you are doing. Most likely, your life and business are not in harmony and may need a course correction.

So be bold, be polarizing, and cause some controversy!

Chapter 7

Getting the Respect You Deserve

We just talked about causing controversy, which is all about getting attention. Now, let's look at respect. Whether consciously or subconsciously, when people meet you or get to know you, they are assigning some kind of success number to you. This number typically represents your level of influence, credibility, and accomplishments. You can visualize the number being either a range of 1-10 or even 1-100 with the highest number being the best number possible.

People instinctively know that most individuals never change, so it is really hard to get people to see your improvements or level of success going up.

Let's use a scale of 1-10. A number of 1 might represent the guy holding a sign on the exit of the freeway, and 10 might represent Oprah on TV. If someone meets you and after a few minutes, sees you as a 4, with the right set of new accomplishments, you might be able to get them to see you as a 5 or maybe, just maybe, a 6. But they are not likely to ever see you as a 7 or higher.

When your success rises, you want to meet new people at your new level of success. Being seen as more successful is very important. Influence is powerful.

The people who know you the best or have known you the longest are the toughest on whatever number they have assigned to you. The good news is that if you are really screwing up in life, they typically will always love you and see the best in you. The bad news is that if you are gaining a lot of success, they most likely will still see you as just a sibling, the boy/girl next door or that kid they grew up around.

When it comes to business, you need to travel and even sometimes move to break into new groups and be seen for the success you really have become. Just remember that wherever you go, you will take you with you. You should never be running *from* something; rather you want to be speed walking *to* something.

I'll give you an example. After losing millions when I was younger, I had to start over and reinvent myself. One thing that was working was my AM radio show in multiple states. A software company found me from my show and contracted me to help grow their company by traveling around and speaking on stages selling their technology to small business owners. (I did a lot more than this, but you get the idea.)

When they met me, I had just come off the worst year of my life. I'm sure the number they assigned me was not great, although it was good enough for them to see some potential. After close to a year there, it became clear to me that even though no one was generating more revenue than I was, they would never see me as the number I was becoming or believed I could become. Furthermore, when people met me as a speaker promoter for this software company, the number they assigned me was also kind of limiting.

From there, I became the CEO of a very famous marketing company. I did that for about a year too, but that title and brand also came with a limiting number. Of course, this CEO position gave me a higher number than the speaking position I had before.

From there, I went out on my own, but I stayed in the same geographical area and around the same people, so I was still seen the same way because, again, it's hard for people to recognize your improvements and your trend to move up.

As I traveled into new areas, I got more love and respect as I was seen as the expert. The people I met while traveling saw me for the increased success I was then, rather than the number I was when I first went to work for the software company or when I was the CEO of a well-known marketing company.

Of course, when I was back home, not much changed.

Eventually, I moved to California, where I had new first impressions, relationships, and opportunities as the success I had become over the previous years. California's a big place with lots of new people.

I made some power plays, increased my level of accomplishments, and some people who knew me when I first moved to California saw me as more, but they didn't do so as easily as the new people I met along the way who saw only my most recent successes.

Then I started traveling to Australia, and those people gave me an even higher number. They saw me averaging one TV appearance a month, all my books, all my client testimonials, and all my big-time (sometimes celebrity) clients. They were even more excited to get to know and work with me.

Do you see where I am going with this? If you want to grow fast, be recognized for your best work, get more respect, have more influence, and change more lives, then you need to move and travel into new groups from time to time!

Increasing your level of knowledge, expertise, and success is only part of becoming more influential. Pardon the crude metaphor, but you need new blood. You need to get outside of your incestuous local groups, you need to travel to new areas as the expert being brought in, and you need to be introduced as the best of your successes.

Even with so much opportunity in my state of California, I continue to find new opportunities through fresh spheres of influence that people bring me into in places like Salt Lake City, Tampa, Chicago, New York City, Dhaka, Sydney, Melbourne, and Brisbane.

And something interesting happens when you travel more to serve other areas too. It reinvigorates your local connections as well because of supply and demand.

How you are positioned and postured with new leads and opportunities is extremely important. Don't let friends, family, local egos, and those closest to you unintentionally trap you with their beliefs, expectations, and limitations of your success.

Grow your accomplishments and success, and then find new people and places to share it with. This is how you grow exponentially in shorter periods of time.

Chapter 8

Your Mom Was Wrong

We've been examining a topic here that really comes down to what people think about you.

Were you ever teased or picked on as a kid? Most all of us experienced some kind of negativity growing up. Maybe someone made fun of you for trying, maybe someone made fun of you for failing, or maybe someone made fun of you out of jealousy.

Of course, what did your mom say?

If she was like ninety-nine percent of all mothers out there, she told you not to care what other people think. I'm sure you have heard lots of your friends say the same thing. I'll bet you have also said more than once in your life, "I don't care what people think."

But that is wrong. Your mom was wrong...or at least partially wrong.

You HAVE to care what other people think in life, especially the right people. Even more important, you have to care what the right people think about you in business. It *does* matter! (Just remember there is a difference between caring and letting it get you down, depressing you in some significant way.) I know we all want to say, "I'm just going be me, and the world has to deal with it," but that's a fantasy land of failure.

Yes you need to be yourself, but there are many ways to share the multi-dimensional being that you are. Why do you think marketers split test ads, campaigns, and products? Why do you think companies enlist focus groups, surveys, and reward feedback? It is because they know that other people's opinions matter!

How we dress, the words we use to communicate, and the attitude we present to the universe make a world of difference. It does matter what others think, and to say it doesn't matter is to live with a life-limiting belief.

Do we care what the haters of the world say? Not really, but if a lot of them are saying the same thing, we might want to listen in order to learn more about how we might improve.

Do we care what the failures of the world say? Not really because we care most about those people who have achieved what we wish to achieve. But we can learn from the failures of the world, all the same.

This isn't selling out; rather, this is selling up. The experiences people have with you and around you matter. People's opinions of you, and especially your organization, ultimately determine your brand. You must decide what your core attributes and beliefs are that can never be changed, as well as the things that can be improved upon, changed for the better, and enhanced for a better message-to-market match in your industry.

Every time we get defensive and caught up in the thick of things because we can't hear the truth in what someone else is saying, we stunt our growth and limit our opportunities. More times than most people realize, we should care what other people think. You can learn a lot from others if you listen and evolve through wisdom.

Grow thicker skin, listen to what people say, and try to learn what you can. Because it does matter.

Chapter 9

Testing Your Icon Status
What's Your Number?

So now you've accepted that what people think about you does matter, and you know there are ways to change what they think. Before we go any further, you need to know where you stand at this moment. That's why I have devised three tests to give you an accurate view of where you are, and where you need to focus your energy in order to reach your Icon status.

Your Icon Influence Factor

You need to know just how influential you really are. Influence can be a funny thing. You can actually accomplish more when you understand people's Influence Factor.

Want to know your number—your Icon Influence Factor number? Answer these questions below. If you value each answer from 1-10, with 10 being the strongest "yes," you will have your Icon Influence Factor. (There is a more scientific way to determine this, but this is the quickest and most simple way for the purpose of a quick read.)

1. Are you knowledgeable in general or specific answers? Having the answers is important.
2. Do you have a following, a group of fans, or a lot of powerful friends? Who you know is essential.
3. Do you have the ability to make or save someone money? The more money, the better.

4. Are you intriguing, fascinating, and cool in some unique way? Sounds odd, I know, but it's the Power of the Peacock.
5. Do people copy you when it comes to food, dress, music, or movies? The cool factor relates to the Icon Influence Factor.
6. Are you healthy? Health can be sensed by others and has been valued forever.
7. Do you have high energy, charisma, and the ability to make people laugh? The ability to entertain is valuable.
8. Do you have money? Money buys almost everything, and someone who has it can do a lot.
9. Are you good with technology? Quite simply, it is its own language, and those who can speak it have a future.
10. Are you an effective communicator? You can't have everything, but if you can't sell your ideas and listen to understand, you're useless.

It's pretty respectable to be in the 70s, and your number can be relative to your geographic area, or even your industry. People like Oprah, Trump, Cuban, Orman, Robbins, Gates, Jolie, Buffet, and Branson rank in the 90s. These people are on my Icon Power Rankings list.

Influence also has a lot to do with what you can do for others. The more you can do for people, the more influential you are. People will listen to and follow people of authority. That authority can be earned through your accomplishments, given to you through a connection, or in some cases purchased with money.

I believe most of society is only in the 30s and 40s. Sorry, society.

People with higher numbers very rarely follow people with lower numbers, or at least not for very long. As leaders, we often need to recruit people while on our journey to greatness. Just know that if you want to lead leaders, you must have a high Icon Influence Factor. Otherwise you are just leading losers. Kind of harsh, huh? The truth is that people are never losers or failures. Losing and failing are events;

they are not people. Unfortunately, sometimes people come to accept these states of losing and failing if they go on for too long.

You know the saying: "It's hard to soar with the eagles when you work with turkeys."

Every person, every organization, and every movement requires others to take action; it all comes down to just how influential they are. Just as your factor can fly up, it can also fall down. Your Influence Factor is a daily work in progress. So what's your number today?

Your Credibility Competency Score

Now let's test your Credibility Competency score. Answer these questions below. If you value each answer from 1-10, with 10 being the strongest "yes," you will know just how you rate.

1. Do you have all the most relevant degrees and certifications to be the best at what you do? Traditional education isn't always necessary, depending on your industry, but how do you rate?
2. Do you have both written and video testimonials? The more you have, the more diverse they are, and the more specific they are, the better.
3. Do you have endorsements from successful people, celebrities, and people of authority? Recognizable people or people from recognizable and trusted places can dramatically boost your credibility.
4. Do you have awards that are relevant to your line of work and industry? Being acknowledged as a winner by a third-party organization is key.
5. Have you been featured on TV in any relevant way? There is something magical about being on TV, even if it isn't entirely favorable.
6. Have you been featured in newspapers? Even though newspapers are dying, or at least changing, there's a powerful emotional trigger to being associated with them.

7. Have you been featured on the radio? Most radio is live, and it heightens the sense that you are a celebrity.
8. Have you ever written a book? Even though it's yours, it still acts as a third-party promoting your credibility, authority, and expertise.
9. Have you ever had an article published in a magazine? The right magazine can make all the difference.
10. Do you have any proof of the results from your advice? Bank statements, financial returns, and before-and-after pictures documenting transformation can be just what you need to get more people to take action.

Again, if you are in the 70s or 80s, you are doing pretty well. Most people are probably half that. No matter where you rank, I hope you can see where you can improve that over time. That's all a part of Cracking the Icon Code.

Your Exposure Energy Score

The test to score your Exposure Energy is pretty similar. Let's see how you do here.

1. Are you interviewed often on TV? Almost anything can be good.
2. Are you interviewed often on radio? Finding these opportunities is easier than you might think and can really help broaden your reach.
3. Are you interviewed often in magazines and newspapers? Adding an "As seen in…" after your name can be huge.
4. Do you get a high percentage of business from referrals? Having people promote you is proof of fans.
5. Do you regularly publicly speak to groups of people? The position of standing in front of a group and educating the room can make the difference in your business.
6. Do you have a large group of people reading your emails? This says a lot because emails don't get read the way they used to.
7. Do you have a large group of people reading your social media

posts? This is becoming increasingly important.

8. Do you and your websites come up under key words and terms when searched online? Does everyone want to see your website or google you?

9. Do you ever participate in Expert Panels? This is generally on stage, too.

10. Do you speak to large groups through webinars and teleseminars? This is a powerful way to reach a lot of people.

So how did you do? Again, 70s and 80s are really good. Even the 50s could make you six figures if leveraged correctly. Exposure isn't the hardest piece of the puzzle, but it's the area that gets worked on the least. A good PR company can really make a difference here. But in the end, it boils down to how serious and how much of a doer you are.

That's what it all boils down to: Doing.

The road to raising your score is paved with pitfalls and rocks. Don't be afraid to fail forward. I recommend you read and sign my Permission to Make Mistakes and review it as often as needed.

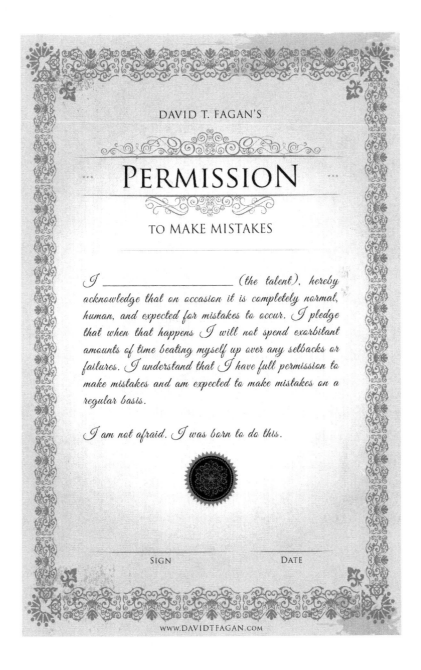

DAVID T. FAGAN'S

PERMISSION

TO MAKE MISTAKES

I _____ (the talent), hereby acknowledge that on occasion it is completely normal, human, and expected for mistakes to occur. I pledge that when that happens I will not spend exorbitant amounts of time beating myself up over any setbacks or failures. I understand that I have full permission to make mistakes and am expected to make mistakes on a regular basis.

I am not afraid. I was born to do this.

SIGN   DATE

WWW.DAVIDTFAGAN.COM

Chapter 10

The Big-Break Myth

Almost every "overnight success" was years in the making. Some breaks are bigger than others but the idea that it happened in one moment all at once is rarely the case. There is an internal power that comes from knowing that success comes in increments.

In 2008, a software company contracted me to a year's worth of business building work after hearing my radio show. This is where I met Roger Salam with the Winners' Circle who referred me to do some work for Harry Dent. Harry took me to a Joel Bauer event where I met Lynn Rose. I later reconnected with Lynn at Larry Benet's event. Lynn then referred me to Diana Wentworth to do some work, who referred me to Steven Memel. Through Steven, I met Lilly Dawson, who put me face to face with Eva Mendes at a Hollywood event.

The day I met Eva was a pleasant surprise. I didn't set out to meet her, but when you get to know good people you will often be surprised at where you end up. Who will you meet today?

Here are some even more empowering questions to ask yourself:

1. Who do you now know?
2. Who do you now know who knows who you want to know?
3. What can you do for others?

Eva was very down to earth, and here are some things I learned (or relearned) listening to her.

As a kid, she performed Jackson songs, and her brothers would shine ·

flashlights on her for spotlights. Her family wasn't poor, but they rode buses a lot in Southern California. She sometimes sat looking out the window at the nice houses and dreamed about the people who lived in them. She now lives in one of the houses on that same bus route.

Some of her big lessons were, "Don't mind being a backup or a substitute. Remove your ego. Take the stuff that other people don't want. Get outside of your comfort zone."

Exciting as her career has been, it didn't happen overnight. She was insatiable, never satisfied with where she was. Like a lot of other successful people, for her, success came in increments.

One of her first successful increments was when some people saw her picture in a photographer's portfolio and wanted to hire her. Another early boost was being in *Children of the Corn 5*. She got another increment when she landed two scenes in the movie *Training Day* with Denzel Washington. Being in the movie *Hitch* with Will Smith was another major increment. It's one of the most successful movies about an interracial couple of all time.

I'll never forget sitting in a room with about twenty other people listening to her talk about her secrets to success. One person asked about her big break. It was something like, "What was your big break, the big moment that changed everything?"

I loved her answer.

She said she essentially didn't have one. Rather, it was a series of smaller breaks. After all, what moment could she single out? Being nominated for an award? Playing opposite Ryan Gosling, Mark Wahlberg, or even earlier on in her career co-staring with Will Smith? Maybe it went all the way back to when she was discovered after that modeling shoot where someone noticed something special in one of her pictures.

"WHAT YOU GET BY ACHIEVING YOUR GOALS IS NOT AS IMPORTANT AS WHAT YOU BECOME BY ACHIEVING YOUR GOALS."

~ GOETHE

www.DAVIDTFAGAN.com

The simple fact is that most of us never really have one big break. It's usually a series of hitting and cracking the glass of success until it eventually shatters. (Of course the cracking comes before the shattering, and there is almost always another bubble to start breaking.)

So what was my big break? Was it being on the *Today Show* with Matt Lauer, *Fox and Friends*, the Sunday Edition of the *Washington Post*? Or was it buying a Beverly Hills PR company that had represented 58 Academy Award Winners, 34 Grammy Winners, and 42 NY Times Bestsellers? Maybe it was when we landed some of our biggest celebrity clients.

That being said, if I was forced to choose just one big break, it would have to be the moment I became the CEO of Guerrilla Marketing. No person besides Jay Conrad Levinson and no education beyond Guerrilla Marketing have ever seemed to have served me so well. But even then that opportunity came from a big break I got from Infusionsoft.

The knowledge I gained from working side by side with Jay, the former Creative Director of Leo Burnett's ad agency and the Father of Guerrilla Marketing, was priceless. The chance to co-author books with him was second only to the knowledge and experiences I received while working alongside him.

Of course, I had to be prepared for the opportunities that came my way, and so do you. My favorite definition of success is when preparation meets opportunity. Have you experienced opportunities you were not ready for or prepared for? Frustrating isn't it?

That's why you have to practice more than you play. That's why you have to put in the hours, work hard, and be on the lookout for the right opportunities. You have to know what a good opportunity even looks like. That can take some time and experience as well.

The truth is, I have to agree with Eva. Success comes in increments. First we crack what's all around and eventually we shatter it.

Chapter 11

Your Brain and Your Brand

I have done marketing for some of the best marketers in the world. Some of these people you may know about because you have seen their testimonials on my website. There are other expert marketers I have worked for whom you don't know I'm acquainted with because my help for them has been sworn to secrecy.

You might ask, "Well, if they are such good marketers, then why do they need you?" The truth is, we all need someone, and that includes me. The simple fact of the matter is that we all carry around so much junk inside our heads that it is really hard to judge things about ourselves from time to time. We all need that second opinion (or more) because we are just too close to the issues when it comes to our own image.

The junk comes from getting criticism we don't deserve; but even more important, it comes from getting compliments we don't deserve. When this kind of feedback is taken in, we can get all messed up with an incorrect perception of our image in the world.

The biggest problem with the feedback is that it very rarely comes from a qualified source in a structured set of specifications. There is a real art to asking questions, surveying, and creating focus groups. It's actually a billion dollar industry. Just ask the people running for president every four years.

Here are some of the best ways to get good feedback that you deserve:

1. Make sure those you are asking are qualified to give you feedback. You don't ask your mechanic to operate on you, and you don't ask a man what he looks for in a gynecologist. You need to be asking the right people.
2. Make sure that you quantify what you really want to know and look for "Major Rights" and "Major Wrongs". What do people really like about something, and what do people really hate about something? It drives me nuts when people feel like they need to justify their existence in the universe by coming up with some kind of advice for the sake of coming up with advice. Pretty soon they are just stretching for something to tweak when, in all reality, they like what you are doing or have done in general.
3. When you want the nitty gritty, use scales of 1-5 (5 being the best) when surveying people for feedback. 1-10 leaves room for some gray areas. 1-4 is better yet. Make them be really specific about how they feel about something.

We all need feedback when it comes to pictures, videos, websites, brands, books, articles, presentations, and sometimes even how we dress. We all just have too much junk in our heads to go it alone. Get qualified people to give you good feedback.

One effective way to do this is to have someone else who is qualified take the I C E tests in Chapter 8 on your behalf. See if they rank you the same way that you rank yourself.

Stop focusing on the stuff you don't really deserve, and seek out what you really do. The time and money you will save will be huge. Get what you deserve, and it will bring you breakthroughs like you have never seen before.

The next thing you may want some feedback on is your brand. A "Brand" is the sum total of all the experiences people have had with any person, place, or thing (products and organizations are things). Yes, people and places have brands too.

Obama has a brand, Vegas has a brand, Mother Theresa has a brand, Miami has a brand, Elvis has a brand, and even China has a brand. These brands were built over time based on what the majority of people experienced. Of course, key people and media with big megaphones can also overshadow what the majority feels. That's why endorsements, celebrity spokes people, commercials, and regular media appearances are so valuable.

So what is your brand? What are people experiencing with you, your products, or your organization?

Your business would be better if your brand was better. In order for this to happen, you have to go out of your way to interact with people everywhere; you have to share, you have to give, you have to serve and, above all, you have to stand out from the crowd. You must interest people. More important, you must fascinate people.

Sometimes this requires you to be controversial or shocking. Other times, simply sharing personal stories and experiences will do the trick. New concepts, strong communication, and the cool factor all go a long way in developing a strong brand. The method combination you need depends on what you want your brand to be.

People are buying your brand. Again, whether you like it or not, people are buying your brand. So what are people buying from you?

I've dedicated years of my life to making people, places, and things Icons in their industry. Here are two major things you can do to tighten and protect your brand:

1. Develop Your Core Stories—People as a majority want to know your story, the story of your organization, or the stories of your customers or clients. As I've already said, you must record these stories, testimonials, and case studies. This personal approach and social proof goes a long way toward inviting people to experience your movement. More than ever, people want an organization with personality and heart. People don't

want cold, heartless organizations they can't relate too. Video, audio, articles, blogs, social media postings, and Power Point presentations can all help you convey these core stories.

2. Manage Your Online Reputation—More than ever, people go to the Internet to learn about you, your products, and your organization. The good news is that it is very easy for you to put out great things on the Internet—especially if you are doing number one and two well. The bad news is that it is relatively easy for people to say bad things about you, your products, and your organization—even if it's not true. You must continually communicate online and research yourself as if you were a potential client. The world is quickly transitioning from everyone needing a website to everyone needing a really good website that serves as an interactive, ongoing commercial stocked full of social proof and cutting-edge technology and automation.

There are some core ingredients in baking up your brand. If you can figure these things out, you will also end up with a pretty powerful and memorable elevator speech.

First look at your name. Do a lot of other people have a similar name? Do you want to shorten it or maybe even lengthen it? Maybe your middle name is more unique or powerful?

Growing up out west my last name was always pretty unique. Once people were really able to start googling their name, I discovered that not only my first name was pretty common but so was my last name. As a matter of fact, I found quite a few people with my exact name primarily out in the north eastern states.

To this day, I mainly compete with one other David Fagan at the top of the google pages. This particular man with my name lives in Australia and is a world champion sheep sheerer! Please don't confuse me with him.

My middle name is Teancum (long story) and in about 2006, I started using my middle initial. Using a middle initial or making your name the longer version to a certain extent can make your name a little more sophisticated. What name has more character or uniqueness? David Fagan or David T. Fagan?

I don't change my clients' names very much or very often, but I do help them change them from time to time. If you want to make the change stick, you really need to commit to it 100% and get everyone using the name you want.

Your name should still be some version of the name given to you at birth. I'm not talking about Chris Andrews becoming Striker Star, but maybe he becomes Christopher R. Andrews.

Looking at the syllables, what rolls off the tongue, and what is noticeably different are all a part of the equation in figuring out your name as an author, speaker, and expert. You may already be too well known; then any change seems disingenuous or inauthentic. Authenticity must be maintained in any name evolution.

Next, you have to figure out the name of your company or organization. The more obvious things to look at are what names are already taken through corporation filings and what website names are already taken online. Even more than that is finding something that says what it is you do and provides the right emotional trigger in representing your business.

The bigger you get, the less you have to say, but when you are starting out you might need two, three, or even four words in order to create the name of your business.

What was once the *Oprah Winfrey Show* became just *Oprah* and now in most circles you could just say *O*. Her magazine is just *O*. That's how well known Oprah is and that is the power of her brand. All she needs is a letter!

Starbucks Coffee is now becoming just Starbucks because they do so much more, and they want to show their brand power. The same can be said for Domino's Pizza becoming just Dominos.

I've used some pretty long version company names like Icon Business Development or Icon Builder Media. More recently my name has been Icon Coach and a lot of people all on their own will just say Icon. I even get people sending me pictures where they see the word Icon telling me that they thought of me. This is when your brand takes on a life of its own.

In addition to your name and your org name, you should have a tag line or slogan that says what you do in some clever or memorable way. You can have several of these that you use in different marketing materials, but you should have one main one you use most. Here are several I use for my company, Icon Coach.

- Making You an Icon in Your Industry
- Making Business People Celebrities and Celebrities Business People
- Helping You Monetize Your Knowledge, Talents, and Experiences

Keep in mind, people want to buy the result and rarely want to buy the process. Ask yourself if the perceived value of your tag line is high. Would people pay a lot of money to get your tag line result?

For me I would ask, 'Would people pay a lot of money to become an Icon in their Industry? Would people pay a lot to be a celebrity or to monetize their knowledge, talents and experiences?'

Remember, people don't buy the diet; they buy the way they will feel being healthier and looking better. People don't buy tax tips; they buy the peace of mind that comes from doing their taxes right and the money they might save. People don't invest in a publicist to learn better ways to communicate with the media; they buy staying relevant, being featured in the media, and the celebrity status that comes from being publicly celebrated.

Having some kind of moniker can really help too. My mentor Jay Conrad Levinson was the Father of Guerrilla Marketing. Dwayne

Johnson for a lot of years was The Rock. Frank Sinatra was the Chairman or Blue Eyes.

A moniker is another name that references who you are. For business people and celebrities, it can be a sophisticated or memorable nick name. It is typically tied to what you are best known for. It could be a talent or even an accomplishment, but it helps say who you are in a way that separates you from others.

People still reference me as the Former CEO of Guerrilla Marketing, as the Icon Builder, or even in some circles as the author of the Bestselling Book *Guerrilla Parenting: How to Raise an Entrepreneur.*

What are you known for? What have you published? What have you accomplished? What nick name or reference compliments you and separates you from others?

Another effective branding formula is to determine three words that best represent what you stand for, what you want to be known for, or what you most identify with. These three words can all start with the same letter, have similar sounds like an alliteration, or even make up an acronym.

My three words are...

- Inspire—I love to be inspired and I love to inspire others.
- Create—I love to create brands, websites, books, presentations, events, and so much more. I love working with creators. I get them and understand them.
- Perform—I love to perform at the highest levels and want to help others be the best versions of themselves.

Notice my three words don't use any pattern, but here are other sets of words I have come up with for clients after having a branding session.

1. Values, Vision, Victory
2. Awake, Arise, Ascend
3. Purpose, Passion, Publishing

As an aspiring celebrity expert or icon in your industry, you should have a book too. Even if it's a book coming out later, determining a book title and creating a book cover can be very important in building your brand.

So let's put this together and answer the question that everyone asks, "So what do you do?" The answer is your elevator speech and you can pull from what we just discussed and created. Mine might look like this in most social business situations...

"David T. Fagan, I have a company called Icon Coach where we make people icons in their industry, helping them monetize their knowledge and experiences. We sort of make business people celebrities and celebrities business people. I actually wrote a book called *Cracking the Icon Code* even though a lot of people still think of me as the former CEO of Guerrilla Marketing. Do you know of anyone that would benefit from becoming a celebrity expert?"

Do you see how I blended it all together? I can easily add or take away from this to fit every setting. What's even better is when you can get other people introducing you with your carefully crafted and brand filled elevator speech.

This doesn't have to be word for word when you express it or when others express it, but certain parts should be a set soundbite. How you go from soundbite to soundbite is what can be changed, but you should become liquid in talking about yourself and your brand. It should be smooth, easy, and casual.

Remember, if you want to improve your business, just improve your brand! And the best brand you can have is an iconic one.

Chapter 12

Inspire Action in Every Audience

Soundbite: a short phrase or sentence that captures the essence of what the speaker was trying to say, and is used to summarize information.

You don't like long stories or confusing introductions, and neither do I. What are even worse are random thoughts with no point or purpose to them.

Fast and effective communication is the key to success in today's world. This is an art and a skill that needs practice no matter how naturally talented a person is at communicating.

Whether you are writing something to be read or scripting something to be said, your discriminating choice of words is paramount to your ongoing success. The people who memorably communicate with the most impact are those who construct powerful soundbites and segments.

Start with focusing on giving people what they want. Every person and audience have a common theme or interest.

1. When meeting someone new, they generally want to know who you are and what you do.
2. When you are asked a question, they probably want an answer.
3. When you want to learn, you typically want someone to make complex things simple.

You will most likely be talking to a lot of people about who you are, what you do, and what they want to learn. If you ever discover you are going to be saying the same things a lot, you should always find the best and most powerful way to say it.

Especially if you aspire to being a highly paid speaker, author, and celebrity expert, you need to communicate in soundbites and segments.

Here are some of my favorite answers to the question, "So, what do you do?" (See if these answers are short and make you want to know more in a positive, intriguing way.)

- I help people become Icons in their Industry.
- I make business people celebrities and celebrities business people.
- I help people monetize their knowledge and experiences.
- I'm a Celebrity Expert Advisor.

My wife Jill who, as I mentioned earlier, owns a publishing company might say:

- I help people develop their core stories and attract the people they love to serve.
- I'm a Custom Publisher.
- I launch self-improvement and business development books.
- I help people attract more money by creating a Signature Book.

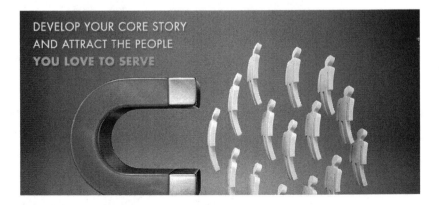

DEVELOP YOUR CORE STORY
AND ATTRACT THE PEOPLE
YOU LOVE TO SERVE

Some of these may be better than others depending on the individual, the situation, or the audience. Regardless, these are all soundbites that, if hooked and bitten on, lead to a longer yet still short segment.

Other soundbites I might use for conversation starters or conversation changers are:

- I'm not a fan of long-term goals. I'm more about Power Plays, things that you can do in three to eight weeks that will make you money or get you results.
- I'm a big believer in customizing your education. A traditional college degree is a waste of time and money for most people. I refuse to pay for that kind of education for my kids.

Turn what you want to say into something short and powerful in the form of a soundbite. Then turn that soundbite into a two- to three-minute segment. Then focus more on how you make people feel versus worrying about how accurately you're describing things.

BONUS: *Find an image to go with your soundbite, and now you have a PowerPoint slide to deliver a segment. Organize your segments in the right order, and now you have a powerful presentation. Learn your soundbites and segments well, and you can create and customize a presentation at the drop of a hat for any audience that may appear.*

If you have ever heard Tony Robbins, Les Brown, or Dan Clark speak, you know that they have these powerful one-liners (soundbites) that just break through to your very soul and engrave an idea upon your heart.

People who rely on networking need to know how to speak in powerful soundbites and segments.

Speakers who want to inspire action in every audience (did you recognize the soundbite?) need to communicate in soundbites and segments.

Even storytellers who want to anchor ideas in individuals needs to use soundbites and segments.

Yes, alliterations and emotionally charged words help with your soundbites and segments. The short sentences should be emotional triggers and feeling phrases that evoke the correct strong feelings that help you communicate your ideas most effectively.

"Practice doesn't make perfect. Only perfect practice makes perfect." ~Vince Lombardi

"The ballot is stronger than the bullet." ~Abraham Lincoln

"Denial ain't just a river in Egypt." ~Mark Twain

"Time's fun when you're having flies." ~Kermit the Frog

All right, that last one is a joke. Still, the quotes that get shared the most are the ones that are short and full of impact from famous people. Can you do that? I think you can. I help people do it all the time.

You have to work on it, think about it, and experiment with these soundbites and segments. Be ready and aware when you say something succinct and powerful, and then make sure you capture it right away. Write it down, type it out, or record it however you can.

I believe celebrity experts make complex things simple. (Did you catch that one?)

Start today and it could pay out profits sooner than you think.

Chapter 13

Content is King

You've probably heard that cash is king...and now people are saying content is king. If that's true, it's only because content is leading to even more cash. Of course, it isn't just any old content that will do either.

Knowledge is everywhere, and in today's world, it's wisdom that people really want.

One of many formulas of success includes being really good at something and then showing others how to be the same. So do you know what you are good at? Can you make someone money or save someone a lot of money? (Actually, you can just be good at research, presentation, and marketing. Just look at my friend Grant and his YouTube channel, the King of Random.)

Here is a crazy cool list of ways to get your content and wisdom out to the world:

1. Quotes (clever things you say that have an emotional trigger)
2. Breakthroughs (share personal experiences)
3. Memes/Posters (combining your words with images where the two together are more powerful than they would be separately)
4. Mind Maps (show the work flow process or organized thoughts in a creative order)
5. Diagrams (my favorite are Venn diagrams that teach in a simple and effective way)

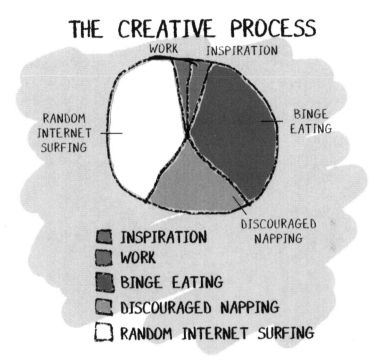

THE CREATIVE PROCESS

- ■ INSPIRATION
- ■ WORK
- ■ BINGE EATING
- ■ DISCOURAGED NAPPING
- ◻ RANDOM INTERNET SURFING

6. Infographics (images, words, colors, fonts that teach a lot with very little)
7. Blogs (thoughts and ideas in plain language that are fairly short)
8. Articles (thoughts and ideas that are a little more sophisticated and structured)
9. Anthology Chapter (when you write one chapter in a book filled with chapters from other experts)
10. Book (a series of framed ideas that teach, inspire, compel, intrigue, fascinate, and at times even entertain)

11. Tests/Quizzes/Assessment (Your info in the interactive form of a test. People love to see how they compare, stack up, and rate)
12. Workbooks (a book that has exercises and tests throughout in order to teach more effectively)
13. Audiobook/Podcasts (Audio thoughts that are structured and shared through listening)
14. Video Presentations (Video ideas, teaching, and entertainments that are structured for the viewer)

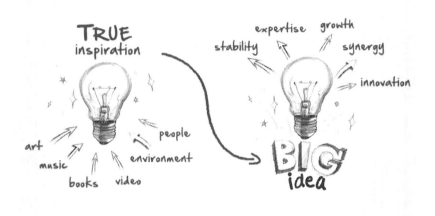

Everything will fit in here somewhere. These components can create powerful informational products, memberships, and certifications. Just two or three of these components can help you develop a following, build a movement, and make easier money.

If you can really develop the first nine components, the book (number 10) becomes very easy!

If you are ever to be a thought leader, an effective author, a highly trained speaker, and a celebrity expert, you need to develop these fourteen forms of Content Creation. Books, videos, and info products in general can be overwhelming. The list above will help you break it all down and create one step at a time.

Try to create something every day. Become aware of inspired ideas, words, and beliefs that you have.

When I say something and see it register with someone, I will pull out my phone and note it inside. This awareness pays off when I need to write articles, author books, and craft presentations. How many great concepts are you conceiving that are just falling between the cracks because you are not aware or you are not recording them when they happen?

Too many, I'm sure.

These fourteen categories can become dots that you start to connect in various orders to create killer content for the world to consume. After all, content is king! Content drives SEO, content individualizes you, content sells your ideas and proves your value.

Just be careful. Creating content is contagious and fun. Sometimes I think I would just rather write books, make memes, and inspire people more than anything else. Content creating is easy when you know how to break it down into simple assignments and formulas.

Chapter 14

The Law of Multiplication

The definition of the Law of Multiplication is marketing and selling one message multiple ways, multiple times, to multiple people. Another way to explain it is cloning your message because you can't clone yourself. It's about taking one lead at a time or one sale at a time and building upon that foundation.

That definition was published in my first book with Jay Conrad Levinson *Guerrilla Rainmakers: How to Make Your Business Rain Profits through the Law of Multiplication*.

Guerrilla Rainmakers not only help their own businesses, but everyone in their association will reap a downpour of profits. Instead of bringing in 100 leads and making 20 sales per month, the Guerrilla Rainmaker helps 20 people bring in 20 sales and a couple hundred more leads each.

In this way, they can literally stimulate the economy alone!

Let's take a brief look at the list of activities and resources you must utilize on a regular basis in order to maximize the Law of Multiplication in your business. Earlier in this book, we referred to these as "Power Plays".

1. Books
2. Audio
3. Video
4. Social Media

5. Radio
6. TV
7. Direct Mail
8. Print Media
9. Speaking at events
10. Fans—Testimonials, Endorsements, and Referral Partners

Why talk to one person at a time when you can reach infinitely more prospects through radio shows, TV appearances, website content, books, direct mail, magazine articles, and speaking at large events? Icon Advisors make the most of their valuable time by getting their messages and sales pitches out through these vital channels.

Every busy person out there jokes about cloning his or herself. The Law of Multiplication, and specifically these power plays, makes this "sci-fi concept" possible.

Even if you only did half of these well, you would be hugely successful, and your business highly profitable. Some people are millionaires just by focusing on one of these areas. Imagine the possibilities for your enterprise if you learned each one of them very well and then used them all on a regular basis.

I have eight kids, run several businesses, write books, travel around the world speaking, coach my kids' sports teams, and am involved in my church. I assure you that I have no more time than you do. So how do I get so much done? It's through living the Law of Multiplication.

Some of the most successful Icon Advisors out there are the ones with the biggest megaphones. Just look at Ellen, Oprah, Rush, and King. They are not talking to one person at a time. The say something once, millions hear it live, and millions more hear the recording.

To be the most profitable Icon, you must learn and leverage the Law of Multiplication.

Another important piece of advice I want to give you is to ask yourself how serious you are about success.

Have you ever noticed the biggest family get-togethers are when friends and relatives pass away? Obviously this is an important time to drop everything and celebrate the life of this loved one. People come from all over, putting their lives on hold and doing whatever it takes to be with the ones they care for.

We prioritize the things that we value most. Some might say that if it's really important, we will find a way, and if not, we will find an excuse. The point is that we find time that we say we don't have for certain emergency circumstances in our lives, don't we?

My biggest books have been written, my best marketing and publicity campaigns have been planned, and my best joint venture events have been executed with the same priority as a death in the family. I know this might sound morbid to some, but you have to know how serious certain events in your life are.

Our money and other material possessions cannot be taken with us when we die. We need to collect moments, not things. We can't be so busy building a business that we forget to live a life. But what is holding you back in your business?

What would your life look like if you finally built out your online presence?

What would your life be like if you wrote an iconic legacy book?

What would your life be like if you were prepared for every major opportunity?

These accomplishments require time that most people don't take because they are too busy. Sometimes you must sacrifice sleep, personal interest, and even time with your family to pay the price that will make you more worthy of super success.

We don't do this so that we will be rich, but so that we will be fulfilled and live our lives to our fullest potential. What is the best version of yourself? Are you developing your core story so that you might better attract those you love to serve most?

It all starts with hard work, service, and sacrifice. Find the time, make the time, leverage the Law of Multiplication, and learn how to clone your message to the world with books, video, audio, social media, platform speaking, traditional media, and through fans.

Take this advice seriously. Choose the thing that will change your life forever, and do it now as if a loved one had just died. Super success is that serious.

Chapter 15

Fans, Fanatics, and the Formula

Fans and fanatics. Actually, the shorter word derived from the longer one.

Merriam-Webster's dictionary defines "icon" as a person who is really successful and admired. I'll add to that and explain that it is a person who has fans. A "fan" is defined as a person who likes and admires someone or something in a very enthusiastic way. Winston Churchill says, "A fanatic is one who can't change his mind and won't change the subject."

How would you like to have more fans and fanatics for you and your business? How would you like to have people who admire you, won't shut up about how great you are, and are enthusiastic in every way about what you stand for?

This would mean you are an Icon in your industry. When you have a clear and defined expertise that you can teach others, you are an Advisor. To be an Icon Advisor is to have the greatest opportunity to leverage fans, win clients, and be profitable.

An Advisor with no audience is almost a waste of time if you want to make money. Being an Icon with nothing to sell is to be a starving artist or expert. The code starts to crack when someone starts to combine these two elements of an Icon and Advising.

The process of first finding new clients and then turning them into raving fans is fading away. Now, we have to make people fans first and buyers second. Crazy, I know, but that's exactly what we have to do in this new digital age of social media and overall interaction. Everyone is doing a lot more homework before they spend their hard-earned money—and they should.

The Formula

I've probably already broken a few brains out there with this new formula. You may be asking yourself, "How do I make someone a fan who has never bought anything from me?" The secrets to the new paradigm shift of "fans first and buyers second" are found in giving. When we add value to peoples' lives and serve them, we essentially earn the right to ask for something. That something doesn't even need to be a sale…at least not right away.

Giving and serving will lead the prospective fan to share more of themselves with us if done right. Notice I didn't say, "Share more information with us." Don't get me wrong. We want people's information, and that is a valuable baby step. But more important, we want to get to know people and interact with them. Two-way communication is paramount in today's marketing relationships.

There is an old expression that goes like this: "People don't care how much you know until they know how much you care." If you want more fans, then open up wherever possible and show them that you care. Reveal the real you. Support or create a meaningful movement.

People want authenticity from their advisors—not guruship. People want to work with givers, not takers.

Some of the best organizations out there have official or unofficial loyalty programs. This may entail all kinds of rewards, discounts, insider info, and special offers through the organization's strategic partnerships. This is great, but the "Fans First" mentality teaches you to have a loyalty-like program before the sale as well as after the sale.

Unfortunately, most people will devalue the things you discount or give away free. However, that's not a reason to avoid this mentality altogether. Instead, it's your job to make sure that there is a high perceived value of the things you give, share, and discount.

Quite simply, you have to stop chasing sales, and start building and maintaining relationships.

In addition to fans, Icons have a combination of social proof and specific accomplishments that separate them from other mere mortals.

Specific accomplishments and social proof include:

1. Testimonials
2. Endorsements
3. Awards
4. Degrees
5. Certifications
6. Proof of Results that came from your advice
7. Having a published book
8. Being published in magazines and newspapers
9. Hosting a radio show
10. Hosting a TV show
11. Being interviewed regularly in the main stream media
12. Being regularly mentioned, acknowledged, or quoted in the media
13. Having made a lot of money
14. Having helped a lot of people
15. Having broken previous records

You do not have to accomplish or acquire all of these things to Crack the Icon Code. However, you need to keep accomplishing a certain combination of these things in order to stay relevant in your industry. More on these 15 points shortly.

Fan Interaction

An Icon Advisor is constantly doing online sales activities or has hired someone to do it for them. Either way, a factor of the Icon combination is to have a healthy online presence and interact with fans digitally.

Fan Interactivity
You & the Fan

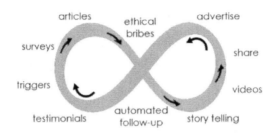

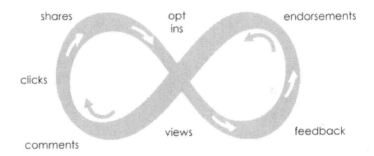

www.DavidTFagan.com

You should be writing articles. I like the word articles versus blog posts. Articles are more associated with value, expert status, and success. You should be surveying people, sharing testimonials, advertising, sharing valuable information, putting up videos, telling intriguing and fascinating stories, and inviting people to opt in or give you their information and permission to contact them.

If this is done well, your fans should be sharing your articles, clicking on your links, commenting on your posts, viewing your videos, reading your articles, opting in, and giving you consistent feedback and compliments.

This is a two-way interactive process of creating activity in your pipeline process. This process can be addictive and misleading as to the actual results of your efforts. But it's necessary all the same; you just need to assign the right value to these marketing activities.

The image above will show you what the process looks like for both you and the fan. Notice that it is illustrated with the infinity symbol. That's because it should never stop.

Part II

Your Icon Solar System

"Complexity is your enemy.

Any fool can make something complicated.

It is hard to make something simple."

~ Richard Branson

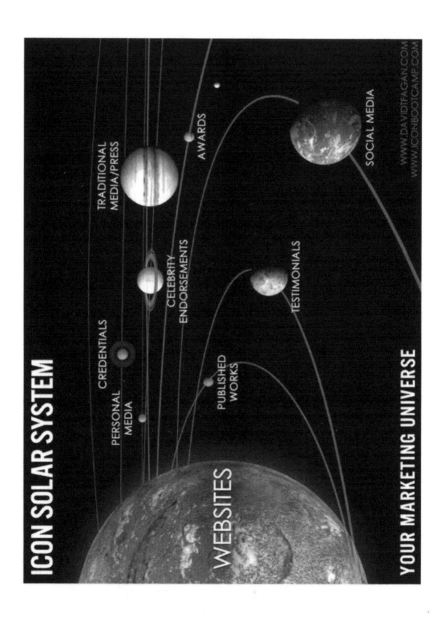

Chapter 16

The Sun in Your Solar System

Websites are the sun in your marketing universe. Everything should rotate around them and be in their gravitational pull. Your website is your storefront and says a lot about your business, whether you like it or not.

We now live in a world where, if you really catch someone's attention, one of the first things they are going to do is google you. Will they find something that impresses them and engages them? Or will they be under-whelmed and uninspired by your lack of presence? If your site is old and outdated, the feeling might be that your information and advice is old and outdated. If your site is basic and cheap, people may think you are basic too, and that you are not successful enough to afford a better image. The Internet is the great equalizer, and we must use it to our advantage!

Websites are NOT "one size fits all". So many people totally misunderstand what their website is really for, how to leverage a good website, or even what a good website is for their organization. For so many of us, a website should be more of a toolbox filled with sales-building tools rather than an automated cash register.

The fact is that people don't spend thousands of dollars on services with trusted advisors without some kind of personal touch or pre-existing relationship. The exceptions are few and far between.

So let's get the big fat exception to all this out of the way. If you are just selling "widgets" online, then this really doesn't apply. If you are in the advice business selling services, then you are the product, and it's an entirely different approach. Your website should then be more focused on saying what you personally shouldn't have to, like how great you are.

An Icon Advisor's website should be a digitally and graphically pleasing resume that hits all the right emotional triggers that scream and echo success. That's why you want video testimonials, written testimonials, pictures of awards, credible affiliations, where you have been seen, and what you have been featured in. This could include degrees, titles you have held, significant achievements, books that you have written, articles that have been published, and radio and TV stations you have been on. All of these will reinforce what results you deliver for your clients, and that's what's most important.

Any first phone call consultation with me will include me giving the prospect a tour of my websites that best apply to their needs. I never want to say anything that could be better said through my websites and the third-party social proof that can be found there.

No matter how little social proof you have, use it to get more—even if it means working for free to get testimonials, successful case studies, or recognition by a third-party organization.

The bottom line is that you don't set up or expect your website to be an autopilot cash register ringing out sales in the thousands daily, weekly, or even monthly. Rather, set up your website to be your 24/7 "sales person" that answers questions of doubt with success stories and overcomes objections with third-party social proof.

Must Haves

In chapters and conversations like this, I always feel the need to start with this disclaimer.

DISCLAIMER: There are no "silver bullets" in marketing.

This means that there is no one thing that works every time for every person in every place. The idea is to always implement as many best practices as you possibly can.

Below are the must haves and best practices for your website. Although some of these must haves and best practices are more important than others, we will keep the math easy. Go ahead and give yourself 1-5 points for every one of these "must haves":

1. Good picture of the product. If you are in the advice business, then YOU are the product. Speakers, authors, coaches, trainers, attorneys, dentists, chiropractors, Realtors, and CPAs cover a fair amount of the industries I am talking about.

2. Third-party images that act as social proof. I'm talking about awards, degrees, media recognition for you, your clients, and your products, and services. Always sell through other people, organizations, and companies.

3. Testimonials that take the shape of both video and written words. Show diverse groups of people in both natural settings as well as sophisticated backdrops.

4. Images that move are keys to catching the eye and holding people's attention. Sliders or carousels do this well.

5. A strong ethical bribe is paramount in capturing people's information. "I'll give you (blank) if you give me (blank)." The more valuable the gift, the more information they will give you. Videos, mind maps, demonstrations, and digital books and magazines seem to have the best response.

6. Have an opt-in and a way to use auto responders. Capturing leads from people who visit your website is a top priority.

7. "Attention Getters" are hugely important, especially when you have a website with lots of information on it. These "Attention Getters" should directly or indirectly focus on what's in it for the website viewer or prospect.

8. Surveys or polls that capture feedback and promote interaction are showing positive results when tracked. Getting people to click, take action, and participate is fundamental.

9. Compartmentalize your website. Things shouldn't blend or be

hard to read. You should be able to glance from area to area and read everything easily.

10. Have Social Media feeds. Having Twitter or Facebook updates on your website allows you to easily and automatically be updating it all the time. It also adds credibility and sophistication to any site.

11. Don't let good sales copy ever take a back seat to "pretty" if you want to make good money.

12. Have lots of images that trigger the right emotions you want for your business.

13. Your message should match your demographic. Age groups, professions, etc. can alter how you might determine your colors, images, and video.

14. Have lots of articles or blogs that people can share, comment on, or even rate. Keep in mind, as I touched on before, that there is more credibility in an article than a blog post.

15. Always put an image or thumbnail next to your articles.

16. Your pictures, social proof, ethical bribe, opt-in, slider, and attention getter should all be above the fold on your website. This means that all these things should be visible to the average viewer on your website, without them having to scroll down.

17. Everything above the fold is your website real estate.

18. Have your website built in a way that you can update as much as possible yourself. If your time is extremely valuable, then have someone on call who can make changes for you at the drop of the hat.

19. Update your site regularly so people feel the need to keep coming back. This is another reason to have social media feeds and post articles.

20. Use up-to-date formats, designs, and graphics. People can tell when you are using something out of date. The better it looks, the better you look—and the more you can charge.

21. Make sure your sites are very specific to a purpose. Selling sites, squeeze pages, membership sites, and main sites can all vary a

THE WEB BUSINESS

PROGRAMMER
The person that writes code typically from scratch to create a new website or to tweak an existing web theme in order to maximize it.

DESIGNER
The person dealing mostly with the graphics, images and over all visual appeal.

COPYWRITER
The person who decides what is written and where it should go in order to maximize interactivity and over all action from the web viewer.

THEMES
Companies that provide more generic website platforms that can be more easily built out from people that may not be programmers or know how to write code. This include Weebly, Word Press, or Joomla.

HOSTING
The person or company that supports and keep the website online. This is usually a monthly or annual service. This could be GoDaddy or Host Gator.

PLUGINS
Smaller programs with a more basic function that just connects to existing websites in order to avoid extra custom programming. This might include IM Chat, Social Media, or Shopping Carts.

SEARCH ENGINE OPTIMIZATION
The person or company strategically creating content for a website so that it might more naturally and organically be found online.

LEAD CAPTURE AUTOMATION
This is the company and software designed to capture clicks, views, collect information, and send information automatically. This might include things like awebber, Infusionsoft, Constant Contact or Mail Chimp.

little. Set your expectations appropriately for your website. People in the advice business who sell big-ticket items for services will most likely never be able to sell online. Your main site, with the checklist I just provided, should be mostly about demonstrating credibility and influence.

Now add up your score and see how you rate on these must haves.

A   91-100 points
B   81-90 points
C   71-80 points
D   61-70 points
F   51-60 points

Here is a bonus item to consider. Do you offer IM Chat on your website? This feature can allow you or an employee to see when people are on your site, what link they came from, and even what kind of computer they are using.

This creates an opportunity for your organization to engage the visitor and interact with them. This is one more way to find a suspect and get them into some kind of discovery process even if the whole thing just happens right on the website with a purchase of some kind.

IC⏻N Building WEBSITES

By *David T. Fagan*

Your website must capture the attention of the visitor in **4 seconds or less**

WHAT NOT TO DO

Copy 39%
What you say through words that explain what's in it for them is paramount especially if you can do it in an intriguing and fascinating way

Images 26%
High Quality emotional charged pictures or story telling images that reinforce copy is huge especially if you want to interact with all of the visitors brain

Spacing 13%
The desing of the site that compartmentalizes idea's and content is important for easy navigation and a good online experience

Homepage Traffic
86% of all web visitors will stay on the homepage and will not click to a back page

Testimonials 11%
Videos of raving fans, written explanations of happy experiences from clients, and celebrity endorsements are game changers

Media References 6%
Don't hide your connections to the media, appearances on the media or features by the press

Fonts 11%
The size, style and color of your fonts matters when it comes to what gets read first, what's most likely to be acted on and how easy it is to read

WWW.DAVIDTFAGAN.COM   WWW.ICONBUILDERMEDIA.COM   WWW.ICONBOOTCAMP.COM

Chapter 17

The Rewards of Writing

If an Iconic website and strong online presence is the sun, and the thing an Icon Advisor needs first and foremost, then the second most important thing is to have a book. It's a marketing planet for sure.

To this day, being a published author holds a certain magic that can't be denied. It is still one of the clearest ways to separate the Icons from the amateurs.

Being published is still the ultimate business card, door opener, and income increaser. Your book is your chance to share your stories, your ideas, and your concepts with the world in a professional way. It quickly separates you from the competition and drastically improves your opportunities to speak in public. A book can give you tons of content for Internet marketing and can give you a way to build a list of followers by providing limited amounts of that content through an opt-in online. Film start, professional athletes, politicians, captains of industry, and scholars all write books. You want to join this elite group of people!

Every professional sports league has an award for the Most Valuable Player. The MVP is the super star individual who is one of the best players in the league, means the most to their team, and as an owner, would be the first person you would pick as the one player you would most want to build a team around.

So what's my Marketing MVP?

When you incorporate as many marketing strategies as I do, it's hard to determine what domino falls first. In other words, what marketing piece or what marketing collateral means the most to my business. After all, I use Infusionsoft a pretty powerful CRM. I regularly leverage social media platforms, speak at events, and pretty regularly appear on TV as a celebrity guest expert.

So what marketing matters most? What marketing do I continue to want to build my business around?

Books! My MVP of Marketing is the books I write, publish, and promote.

SHOULD YOU WRITE A BOOK?

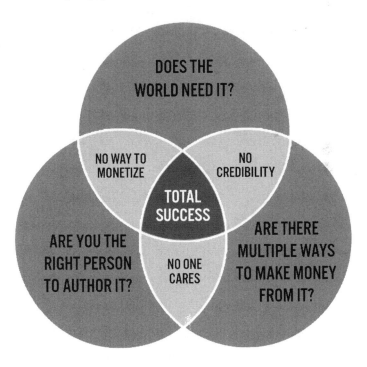

Books have gotten me attention, separated me from the competition, landed me speaking gigs, given me content for marketing campaigns, earned me fans, packaged and framed my ideas in a Tiffany box, and ultimately gotten me on TV programs like *Fox and Friends* or the *Today Show*.

My books leverage the Law of Multiplication by marketing one set of ideas and formulas multiple ways, multiple times, for multiple people.

I have done very well with books, writing forewords for people, endorsing them, contributing to them, and even co-authoring them occasionally. Every book I have ever written has helped me in some way, several of them making me hundreds of thousands of dollars. But it wasn't until after writing several books that I really struck gold. And here's why:

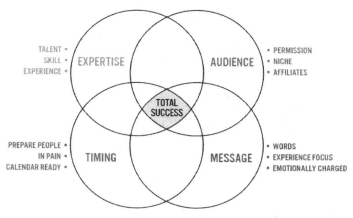

WHEN EXPERTS MAKE THE MOST

YOU NEED TO BE THE RIGHT PERSON, SAYING THE RIGHT THINGS
TO THE RIGHT PEOPLE AT THE RIGHT TIME

TALENT •
SKILL •   EXPERTISE   AUDIENCE   • PERMISSION
EXPERIENCE •   • NICHE
                                                      • AFFILIATES

TOTAL
SUCCESS

PREPARE PEOPLE •   • WORDS
IN PAIN •   TIMING   MESSAGE   • EXPERIENCE FOCUS
CALENDAR READY •   • EMOTIONALLY CHARGED

www.DAVIDTFAGAN.com

That's right, it took me several books to learn how to target all four areas. When you develop the right expert brand, create the best marketing message, get it to YOUR target audience, and do it all at the right time, you really win it all!

I've seen great messages go to the wrong market, and then these people think they need to change their message. What they really need to do is get to the right market. I've seen powerful experts approach people at the wrong time. Then these experts consider changing who they are and what they do, when what they really need to do is time their opportunity better.

A great book done right can open more doors and make you more money than anything else, guaranteed.

Before you ever try to market or sell again, ask yourself about these four areas of when experts make the most. Good is good enough when you are getting started, but in order to maximize every opportunity, you should strengthen these four areas as much as you can.

Yes, we help people with brand strategy sessions, photos, videos, websites, and PR, but books are the one thing that brings it all together. Lead with a book. Nothing else compares or comes close for the time and the money. If you already have a book, then look to improve it. The cover is where most people fall short. Do not skimp there.

Are you ready for a book, or ready to improve your existing book?

Even your book should nail the four areas of when Experts Make the Most. One of the reasons why good people with good content put off a book is because they are overwhelmed by the process and time involved. The truth is you can start to benefit from a book in just a couple of days with a good cover announcing that your book is coming soon.

The Top 3 Mistakes Authors Make

There are a lot of common mistakes in book producing, publishing, and profiting.

Authors DON'T get good opinions early on. Some of the greatest and most successful authors have a "Book Board," which is a qualified group of people who give feedback at various milestones in the process. My Book Board is priceless and generally doesn't cost me anything.

THE BOOK BUSINESS

PUBLISHERS

The organization of record for a book. May or may not do more than this. Random House, McGraw Hill, On the Inside Press, Simon and Schuster, You

WRITERS

Individuals behind the scenesthat may help research and or write portions of the book. This could be ghost writers and research assistants.

PRINTERS

The organization printing the book. May be the Publisher. 48Hour, Create Space, TPS1, Best Book Printing

DESIGNERS

Individuals that design the inside as well as the outside of the book This could be graphic designers on the outside and interior designers on the inside.

AGENTS

Representatives that sell your books to publishers for a percentage. They might be called literary agents or book agents.

EDITORS

Individuals behind the scenes that help improve flow, grammar, story telling, and spelling. They might be called Content Editors as well as other Editor names.

DISTRIBUTORS

Stores, websites and businesses that sell books. Barnes and Noble, Amazon and Marriott Hotels.

PUBLICISTS

Representatives that promote your book along with it's concepts and ideas to the media. This could include TV, Radio, Magazines, Newspapers, Speaking Gigs, Book Signings, and Websites.

Authors DON'T promote their book early enough. It's never too early to create a book cover and start sharing it with the world to gauge feedback, interest, and buzz—even advance sales. My book covers are always shared through social media strategically, and I have been on tons of media about books before they even come out.

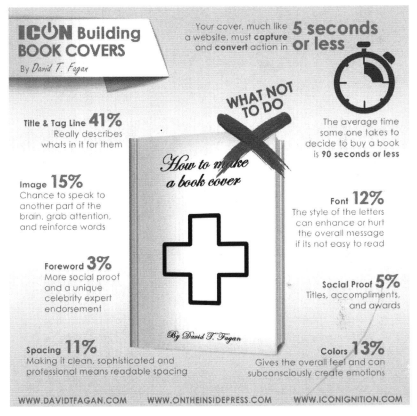

(Exceptions to the rules can be made, but know the rules.)

Authors DON'T plan properly for where the book profits will really come from. Most book profits won't be directly from book sales; rather they will come from speaking, coaching, and consulting. You must plan for this. My books have earned me over $1 million in just the last couple years alone, and only five percent or less has come from book sales.

Do you think that there are more mistakes than just these three? If you said yes, then you are right!

Here are some aspects of books that are often forgotten, overlooked, or misunderstood:

- Editing and Formatting
- Writing Styles and Content Creation
- Ghostwriting Relationships
- Printing and Distribution
- Forewords, Afterwords, Introductions
- About the Author Sections
- Annotations
- Endorsements
- Testimonials
- Amazon Uploads
- The difference between eBooks and Digital Books
- ISBN#'s
- Library of Congress
- Book Titles, subtitles
- Book Cover set up and testing
- Book sites
- Book Trailers
- Anthologies
- Guerrilla Marketing for Books
- Beyond Bestselling
- Interviewing Technology
- Transcription Services
- Group Editing Audience
- Book Sizing
- Book Fulfillment

Are there other combinations of social proof that can move you from amateur to Icon without a book? Sure there are, but it is a tougher combination to unlock for sure.

If you don't have the time to write a book, get a ghostwriter to help you. You can also record an audio of yourself talking out your book and then hire a professional writer to develop it. Another solution for the all-too busy individual is to just write a chapter in an anthology.

Several top authors and experts, including myself, are always looking for contributors to our anthologies. Mine is called Zero to Hero in 90 Days or Less. It's a book of best practices for transformation and getting results from industry experts.

A book like that is great because almost any Icon Advisor can provide a chapter for this type of project. Of course, we don't just let anyone get involved. There is an interview process, and most books require investments to participate.

Imagine just having to write one chapter and having twenty different people help market the book. Jack Canfield, Jay Levinson, and Dan Kennedy have all done something like this.

No matter what, become a published author. Then, if you want to stay relevant, you may eventually want to write another book.

I happen to have some pull with a publisher, and it's not because of my Icon status. My wife is the president of Silver Torch Publishing. One unique thing about her publishing company is that they have a free option to publish with them. You pay all the printing costs, but if a board of advisors signs off on the quality of your book, you are free to use the publishing name so you don't have to self-publish or make up a company name to publish under.

With Silver Torch Publishing, you get a reputable publisher that people can see online. And you're not the only beneficiary. Silver Torch Publishing gets to say they are the publisher of a great book, which increases their odds of attracting more great writers, and the world benefits from another great book. Win-Win-Win.

Printing costs are not as high as you may think, either. Several different online places will give you a price-per-book estimate when you enter in how many pages you will have, the size of book, and quantity you want.

Either way, if you want to unlock more profits and separate yourself even further from the competition, you must become a published author.

In the past you have only had two publishing options, but now it's all changed. There is something new! There are the parents, Traditional Publishing and Self-Publishing, but this baby called Custom Publishing is growing up fast!

Traditional Publishing—McGraw Hill, Simon & Schuster, Random House, etc. These companies have big names and big distribution options so they take a big percentage of the profits, but, in all reality, do very little other than offering their names on your book.

Self-Publishing—You make up and create some company, and then publish your book yourself under that name. This allows the author 100 percent control and 100 percent of the profits. The down side here can be the quality of the books, and the quality of the marketing may generally be low.

Custom Publishing—You pick and choose the services you want for your book, you own 100 percent of the rights, you collect 100 percent of the profits, and you get to leverage the bigger, more successful brand of the publisher.

Traditional Publishing gives you a lot of credibility for your book and your brand, but not a lot of control over your content and commissions.

Self-Publishing gives you a lot of control over your content and commissions, but not as much credibility when it comes to your book and your brand.

	TRADITIONAL	SELF
POSITIVE	BOOK STORES DISTRIBUTION CREDIBILITY LESS $ TO START	BIGGER PROFIT MARGIN MORE CONTROL EASIER FASTER
NEGATIVE	LITTLE SUPPORT LITTLE PROFIT % LITTLE SAY LONGER WAIT TIMES	LITTLE EXPOSURE BIGGER START UP COSTS LESS CREDIBILITY TYPICALLY UNPROFESSIONAL WORK

That's why custom publishing is growing so fast. It gives you both!

Exception to this Rule: Some at .hors have such a big brand in the publishing world and in-house marketing support that they don't need more credibility from anyone else.

As someone who owns a Marketing and PR company, I can tell you first hand that every little thing you can do to separate yourself and your book from everything else is extremely important. Editors and producers in the media have stacks of books sitting on their desks and endless emails coming to them about promoting another author or another book. You have to break through in every way possible.

Editors and producers will look at your cover, they will check the publisher, and they will check you out online...especially the bigger, more reputable publications and TV programs.

Custom Publishers provide a menu of services like…

- Ghostwriting
- Cover Design
- Reviews
- Formatting and Editing
- Copyright, ISBN#, Library of Congress
- eBook Version
- Amazon Upload and Placement
- Post Card Mailing Campaign
- Book Launch/Signings
- Digital Flip Books
- A "Talk Your Book" Option
- Book Webpage

You pay for the services you want.

Just like self-publishing, the printing is up to you, but now you are affiliated with a reputable publisher that has a nice website and a strong history of putting out good books. It's the best combination of both the traditional and self-publishing world!

Just remember, it's not about selling a million books rather it's about how to make a million dollars with a book.

Avg Chapters in a book **12-15**

Avg Chapter Length **9-12** pages

100 8x11 Word Doc pages converts to Roughly **200 8.5x5.5** Book Pages

Common Word Count per book **40,000**

Typical Book Size
8.5x5.5

Avg Page has about **250** words on it

Avg cost per book is **$5** when buying in the hundreds

BOOKS
by the
NUMBERS

Typical page amount is **200**

By David T. Fagan
& Jill E. Fagan

Avg time spent writing **100** hours

Avg time to get a book done start to finish is **180** days but actual time spent is only **200** hours or five **40** hour weeks.

Typically it takes **50** hours to edit and format a book

$5 is the avg price of a eBook

$19 is the avg price of a physical book

Over **90%** of people don't know the difference between an eBook and a digital book

Chapter 18
Social Media Mining

There is a reason why the topic of Social Media is so polarizing and why it has had such mixed results for businesses. Quite simply, very few people can keep up with changes and even fewer people truly understand how media outlets like Facebook, LinkedIn, Google+, Twitter and YouTube really work. I'd even go as far as saying that most so-called experts who may understand the intimate details of various social media platforms do NOT understand how to really use these tools in a consistently practical way.

Casey Eberhart, a premiere lead generation expert, explains it like this. So much of social media is an ongoing party. How do you act at a party?

1. Do you walk up to people already having a conversation and just ask them to buy something?
2. While everyone is holding their drinks huddled in a small group, do you try to sell something out of the blue?
3. Do you try to yell over the music about how great you are?
4. Out of the blue, do you pull out your wallet to show them pictures of your cat?
5. Do you walk up to a group of people and tell them what you ate for lunch?

While none of these things are entirely wrong in the right setting, these social media lines of etiquette are constantly crossed. Some might even say social media was never designed for businesses. To those people, I say, "Neither was the Internet, but look how that turned out!"

The correct expectation that a business owner can and should have about social media is that it is a great way to build a list and a movement. That is, if you know what you are doing. Sure you can sell on these platforms, but that should NOT be your primary goal or expectation. Social media is for mining out the gold and other precious stones. It's a process that requires skill, knowledge of tools, and a little intuition of where to work.

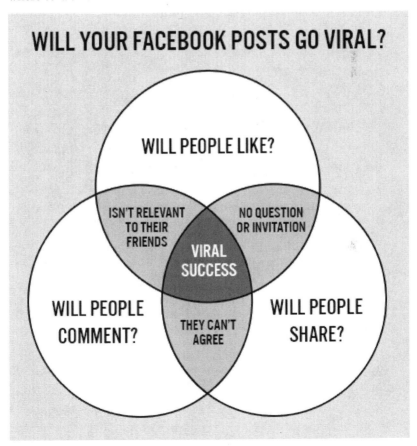

Social media is all about two-way interactive communications. You should gauge your success by how many people take action on or with your posts. If a high percentage of people are commenting, clicking, viewing, sharing, and rating, you have a good shot at being successful. But let's not get ahead of ourselves. Here is the step-by-step way to create profitable Social Media Mining:

1. Create Killer Content—You need to be constantly writing articles, making videos, taking pictures, and making posters for your posts. You have to put out content that is fascinating, intriguing and that will inspire action in the audience that you most want to communicate with. Remember we want interactivity, so we need conversation starters. Your content should initiate conversations.

2. Engage—Once people start to respond to your killer content, you need to engage those people in a conversation. Explore the topic in detail. Go deep. Transform these sometime acquaintances to true friends, strategic partners, associates, and fans.

3. Move Them—Once you are really connecting with someone, move the conversation and the communication somewhere else like a phone call, an opt in where they can get valued information from you or a face-to-face meeting. (Yes, people still meet face to face, and they should from time to time even if it's a video conference)

Don't be satisfied with just being Friends on Facebook or a Follower on Twitter. Create a universe in which people can live in and truly stay connected to all you do. I want my people to connect with me on LinkedIn, register on www.IconMembership.com, friend me on Facebook, come to network with me at events, and participate with me in the appropriate groups based on their interests. I want all their information and want to connect myself to them in every way possible. This is how you build a list and a true audience. This is how you build a movement.

Of course there are many more detailed strategies that can and should be outlined for total success in Social Media Mining. Things like:

1. how to really get people's attention
2. when to be self-effacing
3. what kind of content connects the best
4. how to message
5. how to personalize
6. when to tag
7. how to include people
8. when to embrace quality versus quantity
9. how and when to create a group
10. what platforms are really the best and why some are changing
11. when and how to let other people help you mine
12. how to use images the right way
13. how celebrities and icons use social media

Mistakes in Social Media

Some days are better than others, but if you want more people to see your posts, then you have to post less.

Think of your social media outlets as actual headline news on TV. Ask yourself these three questions...

1. What do others care about in your sphere of influence?
2. What do they respond to?
3. What is newsworthy or even breaking news in your world?

When the big networks get breaking news, it bumps everything else. If that news trends well, meaning people are "tuning in," then they will keep the story going and expand on it. They also don't want to put too many other stories up that might compete with it or dilute it.

The same goes with your social media posts—especially Facebook.

The more likes, shares, and comments you get, the more that post will show up in peoples news feeds. It takes a certain amount of momentum to reach critical mass or the boiling point.

A good post should sit for an hour or two in order to let it find its potential. If you have a post that is trending well and is getting likes, comments, and shares don't give it anything to compete with!

Over-posting is a very common mistake.

Having one or two posts a day that get 50-150 interactions is a lot better than having 5-10 posts getting 10-20 interactions. It positions you and your content better when people are participating, and there is buzz!

You have a brand in your social media, whether you like it or not. People interact with you and have connected with you for a particular reason. When you are true to that expectation of your brand and the reason why people connected in the first place, people will interact more.

Just remember—don't cannibalize your own posts by posting more. You will be eating up any momentum you might already be realizing in an existing post by adding something new to the news feed.

The news feeds only have so much on-screen real estate, so posts compete for that small amount of space. The social media provider is trying figure out (and I emphasize *trying*) which posts your connections want to see most. The ones that get the most traction through interaction are the ones that will show up in the feeds the most, and it starts to snow ball from there.

So don't just think about what you are posting. Think how often you are posting, and how it might affect what you have already put up online.

Chapter 19

Traditional Mainstream Media

Being seen on TV, heard on radio, or written about in print can be hugely powerful. After all, you're in good company when you are highly visible. Visibility equals credibility. Just look at every crazy reality TV show star who goes on to make big money from their new found fame. These people are not always exceptionally bright or sophisticated. However, they are fascinating, intriguing, and they are highly visible.

Sometimes that's all it takes to monetize your knowledge and experiences. The bigger the media outlet, the better! To be able to say in your message and marketing materials, "As Seen On..." is a game changer. Very few people can say that.

You may be surprised to know that the best people don't always get featured in the media. The truth is that most media is a game that is rigged. Maybe you did know that, but do you know how it's rigged? You see, it's all about connections, codes, and creative angles that are skewed to keep out the uninitiated.

As you may know, in 2013, I acquired the prestigious Beverly Hills PR company LCO, previously owned and run by the infamous media expert Michael Levine. It was a seven-figure deal that was featured in the LA Business Journal, and it was quite the whirlwind of new knowledge and introductions.

Some of the companies I've owned have represented everyone from the rock group KISS to Brian Tracy—the bestselling author and motivational speaker—to the Natalee Thai restaurant in Beverly Hills.

Our clients have been featured in Forbes, O the Oprah Magazine, USA Today, Fox News and The Wall Street Journal to name a few.

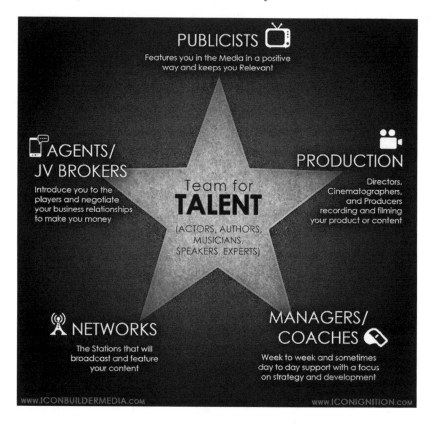

Personal media

It's great to be in the media but sometimes it's even better to have your own media. Having your own TV show (as I do as of August 2015), radio show, or even your own magazine can be very powerful. Having your own media outlets can also make you very influential because of your ability and power to promote others.

The playground that everyone wants to play on. The power of host or editor-in-chief...

Maximize your video appearance

You speaking on video is similar to you writing copy. First, you have to get their attention. Without getting their attention quickly and effectively, they either turn you off or tune you out. Neither is good.

Ideas for getting attention:

1. Wearing bright colors can really help you make your presence felt.
2. Begin with a couple of startling statistics in the form of questions.

Most people want to say "good morning" or "hello" and say who they are, but in the beginning, greeting the viewer really isn't the most important thing. For most videos, where the viewer is seeing you for the first time, you want to start fast and hook them quickly. We don't really care who you are until we know you are talking about something we really care about.

So after we get the viewer's attention and hook them, we say our name...and maybe our moniker or a credible reference to who we are.

Once we have their attention and introduced ourselves, then we need to teach them something in a fascinating, interesting, or intriguing way. This could be a law, a philosophy, an effect, a short story, a case study, or a concept. You could use word patterns like feel, felt, and found. You could use the F.A.B. method, where you discuss a feature, action, and benefit of what you are offering. This is essentially what something is, what it does, and why the viewer should care.

Then you end with a call to action and any rewards or bonuses that they get by taking that action. It should be clear and simple.

Quick Recap of Effective Video Script:

1. Get their Attention
2. Introduce Yourself
3. Teach them something in Memorable Way
4. Give them a Call to Action

Here is an example script.

START

Would you make more money if you were more influential?

Would you make more money if you were more credible?

Would you make more money if you had more exposure?

Hi, my name is David Fagan, the former CEO of Guerrilla Marketing. If you answered yes to any one of those questions, you need to read my book, Cracking the Icon Code.

There is a way to influence the affluent. There is a way to create an unfair advantage over the competition. And it all has to do with raising your Icon status.

This is just another way to monetize your knowledge and experience. I have developed a great brand making celebrities business people and business people celebrities.

Once you learn some of these newer rules that are converting well, you can break them here and there as you experiment with your audience BUT master the rules first!

Here is one more tip. If you are doing a video and really want to start with who you are just say your name first. So...

Don't say "Good Morning. Hi, I'm Sally Smith the CEO of Sweet Treats" or even "Hi, I'm..."

Just say "Sally Smith, CEO of Sweet Treats, and I'm..."

This will seem odd and uncomfortable at first, but I'm telling you that you can leave these pleasantries off and give it to them faster. It sets a tone and feeling of straight to the point.

There are some really easy and effective ways to make your videos inspire action in every audience. Having someone interviewing you or you interviewing someone else is another great way to educate more people and capture more interest.

Endorsements: It's who you know, and who they know

The more testimonials and endorsements you have, the better. Recruit and record as many as you can. After a while, people have to ask, "How can so many people be wrong?"

Train yourself to become aware and conscious of compliments. Learn to respond to these compliments with something like, "Wow, thank you. That means so much. I'd love to capture that on video. It would really help me help other people." Assist people in sharing their positive experience in writing, or even better, on camera. Capturing this is paramount in proving your success. This third-party social proof is priceless. I have hundreds of testimonials, most of which are at www.Youtube.com/davidtfagan. You want testimonials about your work, your integrity, your process, your system, your products, your events, and just about anything else you can think of. Capture and record your compliments. Icons have fans!

Endorsements are what make you look superior to someone with even better qualifications than yours. Start with people you know, those who honestly love your work. Get them in writing. Get them on video. Get them! Then network. Every person you do business with and for is a connection to someone else who can take your credibility to the next level.

Chapter 20

Zero to Hero

Do you want to know how to go from zero to hero as an entrepreneur? So does everyone else. You are not alone when it comes to putting these puzzle pieces together.

The truth is that most entrepreneurs are just happy to follow their dreams going from somewhere to anywhere as long as they get to do what they love.

Most will eventually wear themselves out, lose loved ones, break hearts, and in the end, step off the entrepreneur roller coaster. Only an elite few will focus and break through.

Here is a great formula for going from Zero to Hero in the plainest terms possible. It works in three phases that has a rinse and repeat type of infinity cycle that should never end.

First is learning, then it's earning, and last is investing. Then repeat again and again.

Learning is key. You must know something about the product or service that you want to sell. Sure you can fake it till you make it (a little), but ultimately you should become somewhat of an expert in your industry.

Mark Cuban is known for primarily only investing in things he understands or has an expertise in.

I'm not necessarily talking about college either. There are lots of ways to learn about things. Online courses or even just the internet in general can teach you a lot. Take a class or course that can add to your custom education. Even better, intern or be mentored by an expert. Learning means developing your talents, improving your skills, and looking for challenges that you can uniquely provide solutions for.

Next comes earning money. When you provide a product or service for a competitive price with a unique selling proposition, the money will start to roll in. One thing entrepreneurs learn quickly is that making money is actually pretty easy; it's making big profits that can prove to be more difficult.

An entrepreneur also should earn a credit history of paying debts on time over time. This proven ability can be priceless as a business grows and needs capital to keep getting bigger.

Just as important might be earning venture capital by getting investors to see the potential in their ideas, innovations, and overall business model.

Earning more than you owe is paramount to growth. Saving is just as important. Capital can give you a cushion against tough times and is a huge benefit when opportunities present themselves.

(Earning has almost never been my struggle. Neither has investing. Like most entrepreneurs and icons my trouble is with saving some and creating some cushion. I have gotten much better at this. How about you?)

Once you have more money than you owe, you can begin to invest. You want to invest in both yourself and your business. Entrepreneurs are typically good at wanting to invest in their business with all kinds of tech and toys, but they are typically bad at investing in themselves wisely and investing in their business intelligently.

Take a look at the two diagrams. Notice that the first one is literally an infinity symbol, meaning it never ends.

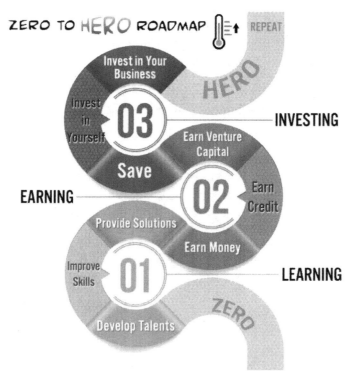

Unfortunately, what makes a lot of entrepreneurs great is also what makes them bad.

The good news is they like doing a lot of different things, so they are always looking for new ways to do things. The bad news is they like doing lots of different things, so they aren't always very disciplined or focused and are always chasing the next shiny object.

The good news is they are not afraid of risks so they will take bold chances going for the gold. The bad news is they are not afraid of risks so they take chances that rarely work out, and they pay the price for it.

You get the idea.

Here are some warning signs that an entrepreneur has a long learning curve ahead of them. They say things like:

1. "I want to work for myself so I can set my own hours." The truth is that a typical entrepreneur is going to work very long hours that may go from 4am to 12am. You also work when clients want you to work or when the industry demands that you work in order to be competitive.

2. "I just want to be my own boss." The truth is that an entrepreneur always has a boss, even if it's the clients and customers he/she sells to. We always have someone to answer to, and sometimes the "be your own boss" mentality stems from entrepreneur immaturity that must be overcome for real success.

3. "I have a million dollar idea." I don't believe there is any such thing as a million dollar idea. I like to say dreaming is good, and doing is better. You can build a million dollar business, but the money isn't in the idea. The money is in the execution of that idea. Entrepreneurs who just want to be idea people are in for a rude awakening.

I never finished high school. I left in November of the 11th grade and got my GED. Later I did take classes at University of Phoenix but never graduated from there either. I also took classes at several other schools including Harvard, where I later found a program for CEO's.

I learned to customize my education, which is what I teach my kids today and what a lot of my book *Guerrilla Parenting: How to Raise an Entrepreneur* is all about. That custom education was an investment I made in myself over time, and I continue to takes classes and courses all over the country.

Don't be afraid to start small, get proof of concept, and never stop learning. Always focus on earning all the money you can, and keep investing in yourself and in your business in every healthy way possible.

The simple fact is that people will typically invest more in their business than themselves. They look for the quick payoff and the easy to see return on investment. (This is also known as ROI.)

You have to invest in yourself just as much as if not more than you invest in your business. Fine tuning your mindset and decision-making skills are drastically important to setting yourself up for success. Never underestimate the power of true wisdom.

Time to internalize what I am teaching you. Ask yourself:

1. How have you invested money in your personal development?
2. How many self-improvement books have you read and reread?
3. How many seminars, conventions, and specific classes have you experienced that focus precisely on your personal improvement?
4. Do you have expenses you can cut so that you can save to invest in your business?
5. Do you have expenses that you can cut so you can save to invest in your personal development?
6. How much time do you spend preparing yourself for opportunities?
7. How much time do you spend looking for opportunities to meet influential people?

8. What excuses do you make for your success or other's success?
9. Do you ultimately feel in control of your own success?
10. Do you know what your talents are and are you developing them so that you can monetize them?

At least a couple of these questions should have really had an impact on how you see yourself. Take some notes and try to capture a breakthrough in your life. See if you can anchor the change you need most.

Chapter 21

Your Inner Mad Scientist

Mad scientists mostly get a bad rap and are the villains in stories, cartoons, and movies. The fact is that some of the greatest minds our planet has ever seen have been mad scientists. Consider Socrates, Aristotle, Sir Isaac Newton, and Albert Einstein.

You must know mad scientists are just insanely passionate experimenting inventors of ideas, solutions, and problem-solving devices and machines.

You may need to ask yourself if you are insanely passionate, or even better, if you are an insanely passionate experimenter. Here are nine questions to see if you have a little mad scientist in you:

1. Do you forget to eat or not care about food when you get a really good idea?
2. Do you forego sleep when you get a good idea?
3. Do you forego sleep when you feel you are close to a breakthrough?
4. Do you chart your successes and failures?
5. Do you research the successes and failures of others?
6. Do you have a "lab" where you can work uninterrupted?
7. Do you love to experiment and try new things?
8. Do you get upset and even more focused when people get in the way of your experiments?
9. Do you have an evil laugh when your best ideas manifest themselves?

All right, the last one isn't necessary, but it doesn't hurt either!

I regularly try different techniques, stories, exercises, and environments when it comes to my events. My team is always playing around with new technology and systems.

Just because you don't use chemicals, machine parts, and electronics doesn't mean you can't be a mad scientists. Every business owner needs to be mad or passionately insane. You need to climb far out on those thin branches—not far out enough to break them, but out there just the same. Every business owner needs to be a scientist or an experimenter.

Oprah, Donald Trump, Mark Cuban, and Michael Jordan are all experimenters who are passionately insane. Look at all the things they have tried...and they are NOT always successful either. They don't just invent new ways to do business or make money; sometimes they reinvent themselves.

Experiment. Blow things up if you have to. Think outside the box. Get outside your comfort zone. Find something so compelling and intoxicating to work on that you lose track of time, forget to eat, have no need to sleep, and just get totally, absolutely lost in your work. After all, is it really work if it's your passion? A mad scientist doesn't think so.

Chapter 22

Launching and Learning to Adapt

5 C's of Launching

1. Conception

2. Collection

3. Creation

4. Campaign

5. Connection

www.davidtfagan.com
© David T. Fagan 2011

Here are the 5 C's to launching any worthwhile Icon Building project.

1. Conception—You need to ask what the unique selling proposition of the company, product, or service is. How is it different from other organizations? It should set itself apart in at least two of the following: Speed, Quality, and Price.
2. Collection—You need to round up all your pictures, images, copy, information, testimonials, endorsements, awards, video clips, etc.
3. Creation—Now that you have collected everything you need, you can create your website, your book, your presentation, your magazine, your videos, convention exhibit, etc.
4. Campaign—Now that you have something created, you can go share it with the world. You can recruit affiliates to spread the word, talk about it in social media, send out emails, and run ads.
5. Connection—Now that you are sharing your business in various ways, you can "poll the audience"; survey people and find out if you are under promising and over delivering. Maybe you need to collect more, tweak your creations, campaign more or differently, and then see if the connection is better.

All of these require changes and the ability to adapt. Can you name the man who has influenced five industries in the last twenty-five years? The man who revolutionized computers, Hollywood, music, retailing, and wireless phones? It's none other than Steve Jobs. He adapted and changed with the world to continually capitalize on markets. He made Apple the only contender to stand next to Microsoft, lifted Pixar past Disney, created new retail stores, oversaw iTunes, and launched the iPhone, which is still the fastest-growing wireless technology. Most would be satisfied to be an expert or pioneer in just one of these areas.

You'd never hear Steve talking about the way it's always been done, tradition, or the impossible. He truly saw change as opportunity. As a matter of fact, if things didn't change, he would have never been able to capitalize with new products and services.

When I was growing up, my family moved around a little. I went to two elementary schools, two junior highs and two high schools. Not as much as some, but it seemed like a lot growing up. I had to learn to adapt at very intense times in my life, and I didn't do as well as I think I could have. I know I would have been a lot happier if I had figured that out at a younger age. My kids have moved even more than that. Making new friends and letting go of old ones can be tough.

Later on in life, I had to go through company mergers, swings in the economy, and a growing family. I can't imagine what would have happened if I hadn't focused on making the most out of each.

I constantly tell my audiences and clients they have to embrace change and look for ways to adapt faster than anyone else. They know that the person who can change the fastest, rather than fight the powers that be, will have the greatest opportunities.

Change isn't easy. It requires us to get outside our comfort zone and think differently. Old habits that were once good can now be costly, but hard to break.

One of my favorite exercises at my events is to have the audience pair up into teams of two. I then have them face each other and absorb how the other appears to them. After they get a good look, I have them turn back to back and ask them to change five things about the way they appear. There's only one rule: don't get naked on me!

Then I have them turn around and look at each other again. After a moment of laughter (because of course everyone looks ridiculous), they take turns pointing out the changes in their partner, hoping to catch all five. After about thirty seconds of reviewing the changes, I have them turn back to back again. Then I tell them to change five more things about the way they appear. There is usually some grumblings, and I write down some of what I am hearing. Things like, "No way," "Too hard," or even "Why are we doing this?" Next it's turning back around, more laughing, and more counting the changes.

Then I have them go back to back one more time and I tell them that now I want them to change as many things about the way they appear as they can. Obviously, there is some more grumbling. At this point, I pull out a crisp $100 bill and announce that I will give the money to the person who can change the most things about the way they appear, which usually energizes a fair number of them.

After a few minutes, it's back to face-to-face and counting. When it's all done, and the money is paid out, I ask what the exercise is all about. I usually hear things like "observation" and "creativity." Eventually I'll hear "change," which is really what it's all about. We then have a conversation about why change is so hard. I'll review some of the responses I heard, and the fact that some of them were too cool for school and didn't even try.

I also talk about what happened when I introduced money and the role it played. Of course for some, $100 wasn't enough to stretch them or motivate them to potentially humiliate themselves. I also ask the same people who did really well at the exercise how they did it. Many will say they looked at what other people were doing; they were only able to come up with so much, but seeing others gave them other ideas on ways to change their appearance.

I'm going to tell you what I tell them at the end of the exercise: there is a lot of money out there for someone willing to change. It takes creativity, stepping outside your comfort zone, and maybe even making a fool of yourself. For those willing to adapt, change, and take some calculated risks, there is a lot of money indeed.

Need a reason to change? Keep reading.

Chapter 23

Why Most People Fail

In the last chapter, we talked about the importance of doing. In this one, we are going to take doing to the next step, one that if you miss, can lead you to a fall.

You, like many, may believe the reason most people fail is because:

1. they are underfunded (yes, that is a good one)
2. they are under committed (yes, that too)
3. they don't take enough action (that's closer)

These are all good, but I'm seeing something even more vital to the success of the average individual looking to break out as an entrepreneur. In order to understand the answer more completely, you must realize that most people are not just limited by their financial resources but also by their internal energy to take consistent action long enough to see the fruits of their labors.

These internal energy limits are not typically determined by the hours they spend working in their chosen business but by the number of days they spend with what they consider working in their chosen business.

The number one reason why people fail is they don't make the effort to collapse time frames and work harder up front.

Let me explain.

One of the many 80/20 rules is this: It takes a space shuttle about eighty percent of its fuel to leave the earth's atmosphere, but then it can make it all the way to the moon and back home again on the twenty percent of fuel left.

That's the way it is for business. That initial breakthrough leaving the earth's atmosphere is always the toughest, and a person needs to look at it in the terms of hours needed to be spent doing the right things versus the number of days it takes to do the right things.

Somebody might say they have been working in their business for a year, but upon further investigation, you might discover that in that year they may have worked only 100-200 hours in the business. That's just not long enough! You must reach critical mass faster!

Malcolm Gladwell says it takes 10,000 hours to greatness, and I believe that it's only 500 hours to profitability. The question is how fast can you put in the right, powerful 500 hours? If you spread out those pivotal 500 breakthrough hours over the course of years, you will grow weak, the world will doubt you, and you will most likely quit like the many others who failed before you.

Can you overcome this average number of why most people fail and do it the long hard "never give up" way through years of trial and error? Yes, of course you can. Or you could just put all the odds in your favor and really go for it!

Carve out 90 days. Find huge chunks of time and commit to the work that needs to get done. Collapse timeframes and find financial success faster. You can't just be doing busy work. You have to prioritize the best business practices but this book is not about those daily and hourly activities.

Once profitable, the game changes, momentum seems to swing to your side, and the world seems celebrate you more instead of challenging you all the time.

You can only procrastinate so much, but you would be better off to save up some energy, organize your efforts, and launch in 90 days rather than just shooting short explosions of energy that don't add up to anything quantifiable.

Yes, there are ways to succeed and plateau, succeed and plateau, and keep repeating that process until you reach total success. I suppose it is better than nothing, but the truth is most people fail long before they ever reach success going the long road of short explosions.

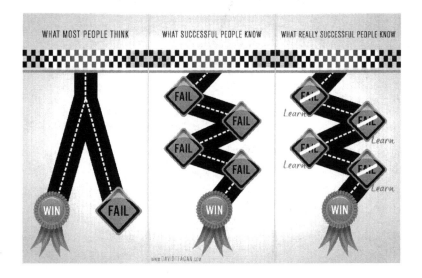

What's worse is that the people who fail on the long road to success are less likely to ever recover. These are the most broken spirits that you will ever see. They basically say to themselves, "Well, I tried for years, and it never worked for me, so I guess I'm not a good business person, nor am I meant to be an entrepreneur." After all, that's what the world would say to that person who tried for so long with no profits.

Of course, the real question is not how many months and years was someone trying to make it work, but how many actual hours did that person spend doing the right things in powerfully short periods of time.

Go for the highly concentrated hours in short power plays! Collapse timeframes and launch with a lot of highly charged hours!

Chapter 24

Power Plays That
Will Change Your Life

I'm not a big fan of long-term goals...especially specific ones. I know this is very different from what most experts believe. Long-term goals have a huge downside that closes us off, limits our beliefs, and leaves no room for new information or enlightenment. Long-term goals should be very generic at best, and all the focus should be on worthy, short-term goals that I call Power Plays.

Ask yourself this. What is something you can do in the next three to six weeks that could get you positive results, make you money, or increase your happiness? Maybe it will take four to eight weeks, but any longer is a waste of energy. Think about a job you want, a position you want, a client you want, and go from there. Think about a book you want to write, weight you want to lose, or a business you want to start, and go from there.

So many people will tell you to plan out big, lofty goals over the course of years and then backtrack. You want options, you want opportunities, and you want to leave room for new revelations to inspire you. You don't need to lock yourself down to something long term; just start.

So many people will wait for the perfect time, the perfect place, and the perfect people. Sure, sometimes you need to temporarily choose a major for college or a career path, or even what kind of business you want to start out in. But that doesn't mean you need to figure it all out now.

I love to sell and provide services for people, but I could do that in a lot of different ways. Real estate was the vehicle I enjoyed most for a decade. I love to transform, taking something from good to great. I have helped someone in the gym, fix up a house, or even fix up a business, and in every example, I could show a before and after of transformation.

One problem with picking big goals is that most the time they won't work out. Every time they don't, you lose a little more confidence in yourself, as if you did something wrong. Maybe you did, but most likely you didn't. There are other forces at work here in our lives. When we align what we want with what God wants, we are invincible. Sometimes it is more left up to us. Other times, it just isn't up to us.

We should always strive to finish. As I'll discuss in more detail later, happiness is finishing. If you want more happiness, just finish more of what you start. That's knowledge, but here is some more true information. Quitting is the secret art of winning.

The fact is that we have had the "Quitters never win" mentality drilled into us for so long through so many books, speeches, and stories that we may forget that it's actually okay to quit.

Maybe you already have this knowledge about quitting. Of course, real wisdom is when people know when to apply best practices appropriately.

Here are a few people who know how to do it well:

1. Oprah quit radio and went on to TV.
2. Michael Jordan quit baseball and went back to basketball.
3. Ronald Reagan quit acting and went into politics.

We can't quit everything all the time. Happiness is finishing, but it's also finishing the right things. The path to finishing the right things many times starts with quitting the wrong things.

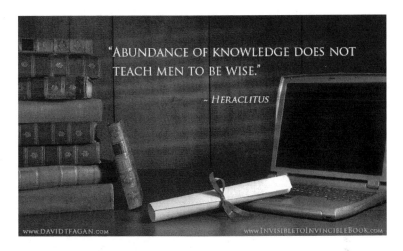

"ABUNDANCE OF KNOWLEDGE DOES NOT TEACH MEN TO BE WISE."

~ *HERACLITUS*

www.DAVIDTFAGAN.com   www.INVISIBLETOINVINCIBLEBOOK.com

Quitting may sound easy too, but it's not. Try quitting a bad habit, a bad relationship, or even a mediocre business. It's easier said than done...and you know it, don't you?

The best way to quit a project, a job, or even a business is to give it a set amount of time and evaluate everything only at that set time. Quitting is most dangerous when it's done in the heat of the moment. Quitting after a bad day, a bad week, or even a bad month is rarely right.

Give it three months, six months, or even a year before deciding whether or not you will quit. Make s' re that you are not running from something (like hard work) and that you are running toward something—a better, more proven opportunity.

Define success in everything that you do. Know what it looks like. Understand what the metrics are in the area of life and business that you may want to change someday. Then, and only then, monitor those metrics with predetermined timetables where you will reevaluate everything.

Don't ever just keep going for the sake of a "never say die" attitude. Some people have this romantic notion of going down with the ship, but that is rarely the right thing. Finishing is happiness. Finishing the right things is long-term, sustainable happiness that comes from learning the art of quitting!

A power play means turning up the heat and getting laser focused.

Are you tempted to push the limits and take on more than you can handle? How many commitments have you made? How many businesses do you have? How many projects are in the works? Most likely, it's too many. It's like adding tap water from the sink to a pot of water already heating up on the stove. The more water you have to heat, the longer it takes to boil!

One of my biggest breakthroughs of 2013 was to streamline my companies and say no to things that were outside of my existing brand and business.

So now I'm finally in hot water, and I like it! Sure, I get in trouble pushing the limits here and there, but what I'm really talking about is that my life and my business is more than just heating up. It's really boiling now! Things are actually cooking!

It seems that so many times in the past (I'm sure you don't do this), I would use the machine gun approach of just shooting as many bullets as I could, knowing I would eventually hit something. Over the years, I have moved toward the sniper approach—or even the laser approach—of really getting one important target in my sights, taking careful aim, and shooting in just the right spot.

If you don't have a lot of support, then you have a weak laser. Likewise, if you don't have a strong team, then you're boiling water on a weak burner. On the other hand, the more resources you have backing you, the bigger the flame you can light up under your pot of water. That's how people like Trump and Oprah can take on multiple massive projects and organizations.

Discovering the right balance of heat and water to reach a boil is paramount to cooking up some real success. If things seem slow to heat up, then empty some water. Power Play something specific that will lead up to a magnified life. Worthwhile, general long-term goals are:

ARE YOUR GOALS ACHIEVABLE?

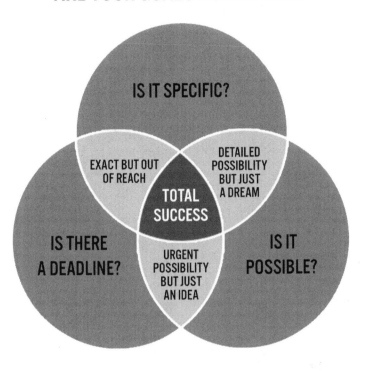

- Saving enough money to live comfortably if you can't work.
- Getting married and staying married.
- Having children and teaching them right from wrong.
- Traveling the world.
- Getting an education.
- Giving back and serving others.
- Getting paid to do what you love.

There are a lot of ways to reach these goals. When we make long-term goals where the odds are extremely against us, we limit our options and our happiness. Remember, you are a unique spirit and a multi-dimensional being with many talents. Happiness is fleeting, and it's the journey that matters most.

Great success comes from many power plays over time. Sustainable.

If you have ever been on a treadmill, you have seen categories of movement like walking, jogging, running, and sprinting. All these numbers are all a little relative, but...

- up to about 2 mph, you are typically walking.
- 2 mph to about 4 mph, you are speed walking or jogging.
- 4 mph to about 8 mph, you are running.
- 8 mph plus is more like a sprint.

You could start a marathon sprinting, which would give you the best start, but sprinting isn't sustainable in a long race. World record marathon runners especially understand this. (Actually, it's this understanding that allows them to set world records.)

The same applies for life and business. If being happy or profitable requires you to always be running and sprinting, then your success is not sustainable. Even if you could sustain those speeds, you wouldn't have time to enjoy the rest of your life. Life is definitely not a sprint.

Watch for seasonal busy times and four-to eight-week power plays where you can really run and sprint profitably. But you also need to find times and seasons in your life where you can focus on family, fun, and adventure.

Are you working insane hours out of true necessity to pay the bills? If so, you can sprint for a long time. But if you are just trying to reach for the next record time in the race of business, then you need to know how to pace yourself.

Choosing the right races, training, practicing, and preparing are all paramount in having a successful running career. The same applies for business. Sprinting through everything is like working and living on red alert. People just can't do that for long periods of time without becoming numb to being on high alert. Besides, once a real emergency comes, it can be hard to find that heightened sense of urgency to give the extra effort.

Don't make emergencies out of day-to-day dealings. You can't call 911 for a paper cut! Learn what you are capable of. Push the limits every once in a while so you can reach new heights, but don't max out in every work out!

Your body must rest in order to rebuild itself stronger after you break it down exercising. When you don't let your body heal and grow, it will become more prone to injury, and eventually it will fail you. Your business is the same way.

We must stop sprinting IN our business or lives from time to time and start spending time working ON our business and lives from time to time. If we don't, it will all break down and eventually fail us.

The last year was full of success as I ran and sprinted my life away. However, in the back of my mind, I knew that eventually I had to settle into something more sustainable.

Here are some ways to pace yourself, pick the right races, and avoid living on red alert.

1. **Have the best team you can possibly afford so you don't have to do everything yourself.** This alone is one of the most life-changing things you can do in your business.

2. **Stay healthy with some exercise and nutrition.** I tell people I sleep fast, and it's true. I have more energy and need less sleep when I eat right and exercise. It's quality over quantity to some degree.

3. **Avoid the panic button.** I'm a bigger believer in tapping raw emotion and laying it all on the line. That being said, I don't go around raising my voice, crying, and laughing until it hurts, but there is an appropriate time for all of those actions. They just

mean more when done at the right times. Don't create a false sense of worry or panic with the people around you. It's like crying wolf. When the wolf is really there, no one will respond.

4. **Celebrate your wins.** I love to go to the movies even if it's only by myself. I frequently go out to a movie or dinner with someone from the office or my wife when we have had a success of significance.

5. **Make sure you know your numbers.** You have to know what it takes to be profitable and then make sure than you can continue to recreate those conditions. If you can only recreate the success while sprinting the rest of your life, you need to work on a new solution for sustainable success.

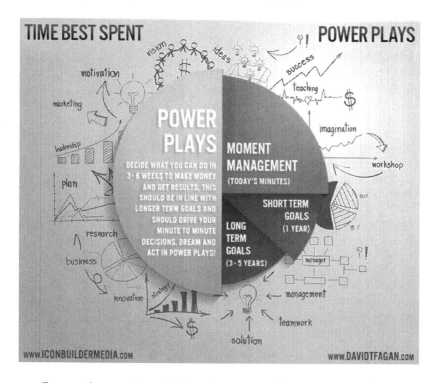

Power plays quicken the learning process because we see the cause and effect of our actions in a relatively short time. Knowledge comes faster. Experiences let us see what we enjoy and what we don't like as much. It can take hundreds and even thousands of hours to really discover a talent or expose a profitable profession.

If people spent a couple hours a week or even a day, it could be months or years before they really know what they want and can really do as a way of making a living. We want to collapse these timeframes in shorter, more effective Power Plays where we really see what we have and what it is going to take to be happy and successful in various areas of life.

You might be in a situation where you have only a few hours a week to try and test something new. If that is all you have, then that is all you have. You have to do the best you can with what you have to work with. All the more reason to figure things out quickly through taking massive action and measuring the success accordingly in short, predetermined amounts of time.

Most of us are more like a speedboat than a cruise ship. Speedboats don't have to be as concerned with long plotted courses because they can turn fast. The Titanic, on the other hand, couldn't turn fast enough, so it hit an iceberg and sank. We must play to our strengths. Be the speed boat. Roll with the punches. Listen to the voice of inspiration. Focus on Power Plays.

Chapter 25

Succeeding Under Extreme Pressure

As a kid, I had a bit of a temper. In the first grade, I had a special piece of paper with a smiley face and a frowny face on it that was given to me for every recess. At the end of the recess, the teacher on duty would circle one or the other, and when I got enough smiley faces, my whole class got a small party. Pretty crazy...and embarrassing, I know.

These days I do much, much better, and my temper is only rarely tested by my kids. Sometimes I don't lose my temper, but I still like to become a little more animated for dramatic effect. (I find that people—especially kids—sometimes need this, and your points can be more memorable with an elevated tone.)

Interestingly enough, some of my greatest successes have come from staying calm under pressure. My team will tell you I constantly preach, "Focus without panic is paramount." As I was writing this chapter, my client, friend, and associate Steve Jennings brought up the concept of constructive tension. Good stuff.

We need to tap raw emotion. We need to feel a sense of urgency and know when to elevate our emotions on various issues. We need to feel all this and more, but this has to be done without losing control of the wisdom we know to be true through our past experiences.

Here are some common things that go wrong when we succumb to pressure and stress:

1. We go for revenge with those who have wronged us.
2. We do what feels best in the moment rather than thinking about the long-term consequences.
3. We forget the big-picture strategies.
4. We cut off our noses to spite our faces.
5. We say something we can't take back.
6. We offer information that can hurt negotiations.
7. Our natural skills and talents are diminished.

The greatest athletes, artists, actors, and performers know the value of working under extreme pressure. The best people seem to actually rise to the occasion, reaching higher levels of consciousness under high stress moments of a lifetime. Although this can come naturally, I believe the best emotionally intelligent people develop this out of a learned ability to access a heightened state of awareness of what is going on around them at all times.

These emotionally intelligent people have learned to recognize feelings in themselves and in others and can then proceed accordingly with an end goal in mind.

I have come to accept and understand that when an emergency of a pivotal pressure moment arises, the best thing to do to help everyone (including myself) is to remain calm and focused. You have to be aware, recognize the moment, and slide into a new state of consciousness that allows you to access only the feelings and ideas that will best help you reach the best desired outcome.

I know. It's easier said than done, but I believe this developed talent and skill has been paramount to my success as well as the success of the influential crowd I have been privileged to associate with.

Are you aware?

Are you autopsying important, high-pressure situations afterward to think about how you did and what you might do better next time?

Can you figuratively stand next to yourself, recognizing the moment and your actions as they are happening in real time?

Success is more than just knowing what to do, but being able to do it under extreme pressure.

Remember, be good enough on recess, and everyone parties.

Chapter 26

The Top 5 Lies We Tell Ourselves

Self-talk is good. Sometimes I need to talk myself down or talk myself forward. Sometimes I do it out loud for more effect. One thing I've learned is that TSA doesn't like out loud self-talk in the security line.

Sometimes our self-talk is really just a lie we tell ourselves which almost always leads to heartache, disappointment, and financial loss. Here are the top five lies...

1. I'm building relationships online. The simple truth is that true relationships cannot be built online. At best, they can be maintained online, but even that is a stretch. If you are hiding behind your computer screen thinking you are just as effective online as out meeting people face to face, you are sadly mistaken.

2. Stuff is happening. People often confuse activity with productivity. These same people often take the foot off the gas pedal too soon, believing their lies of how many great things are going on when in all actuality another unprofitable month is on the horizon. Be careful that you are not just kicking up dust.

3. This will pay for itself. Many poor purchasing decisions are disguised as "investments." The little lie is that you need something, and that you will use something more than you really do. It's been a good ten years since I got really truthful in this area. I lost hundreds of thousands of dollars setting up offices, buying brand new phone

systems, leasing new state-of-the-art copiers, and advertising where my clients don't visit.

4. My time is really valuable. This truth is that your time probably isn't all that valuable. Sure, it's the one thing you can't get back, and that makes your time precious to you, but it doesn't make it valuable. What do you truly make in a month? How many hours do you really work, and what is your true hourly rate? Most people will have a conversation that ends in a sale and that took maybe an hour, and all of a sudden, that is their new hourly rate. It doesn't work that way. How many hours do you spend working that lead up to that sale? How many hours will you work after that sale to fulfill on that product and service? Before you start hiring assistants, project managers, pool people, landscapers, and outsourcing all your sales and marketing wants and needs because your time is so valuable, you had better re-evaluate your true hourly rate.

5. I need eight hours of sleep a night. A sleeping disorder is the best thing that can ever happen to an entrepreneur. With only a few exceptions like being sick or tough work out routines, you can get by on four to five hours of sleep several nights a week and even pulling an all-nighter once a month. The problem is that most people want to party more than they want profits. The problem is that most people want to sleep more than they want success. Wake up at 4 AM, sit up in bed, and start looking at your email. Something will almost certainly start to stir. Maybe it's an anxious feeling; maybe it's even a stressful feeling. Regardless, the blood will start pumping, the brain will start racing, and the fingers will start typing. Three uninterrupted hours of working in and on your business is like working a full eight-hour day. Sometimes social

media, phone calls, and meetings are just interrupting your momentum and creativity.

Just a little self-evaluation. I'm turning your self-talk into straight talk. Be careful about the little lies you tell yourself because they can lead to big trouble. There is no sense in rationalizing your lies and limiting beliefs. Make better decisions, make more money, and create a better life by design. More truth and fewer lies will make you the best version of yourself.

Chapter 27

Icon Oxygen

Any good survivalist will tell you that you need water more than food and oxygen more than water. After all, you can go weeks without food and days without water, but only minutes without oxygen. To ensure that you always have food is GOOD. To ensure that you always have water is BETTER. To make sure you always have oxygen is BEST.

Oxygen is the money in your business. Nothing will suffocate your business faster than running out of money.

Many priorities are important in your business, but when everything seems important, you have to make tough, sometimes controversial decisions as a leader.

When we are in a state of emergency, stranded with limited resources, and on red alert, we must survive by focusing on what matters most. To do so accurately is the difference between life and death in business. (Of course, we should never live in a constant state of emergency. If that is the case, then maybe your business *should* die.)

A drowning man doesn't care about food, and the only water he cares about is the water going down his throat. In this moment, the drowning individual shouldn't be thinking about what got him into this situation or what he can learn from the situation. The ONLY thing this person should focus on is how to get his head above water.

Leads, sales, and collecting money should be the ONLY focus of a drowning business. It's good to learn more about your trade; it's even better to build a world-class team; but the best thing to do is to focus on money-making sales activities when you are fighting for your business life. Ironically, the more you focus on and prioritize money-making opportunities, the less time you will spend on red alert.

Remember, oxygen (money) alone is never enough to stay alive on—let alone thrive on. Rather, it's just one of the top priorities when you just don't have enough time for everything.

Part III

Monetizing Your Icon Status

"I believe opportunity

looks a lot like

hard work."

~ Ashton Kutcher

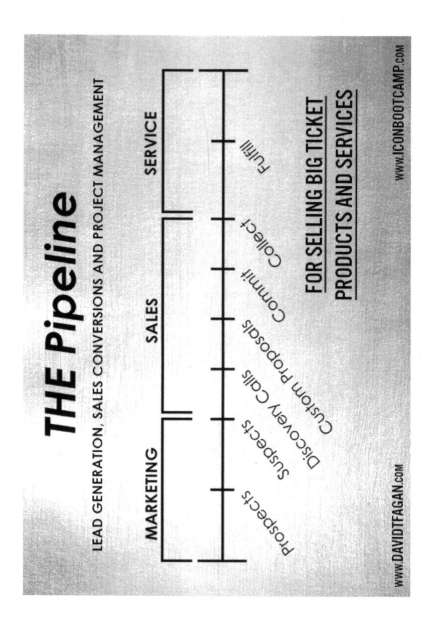

Chapter 28

Introduction to the Pipeline

You have to really focus on various metrics that make up a pipeline of business. This can also be considered your Sales Cycle to some degree.

So many would prefer to just spend all their time chasing sales presentations or people that they can sell right there on the spot. To do that would be short sighted and produce a more average income.

Here is a Sales Cycle worth implementing. I call it a "Pipeline with a Purpose." This is the overview:

1. <u>Prospects</u>—All the people that have been exposed to you and your organization.
2. <u>Suspects</u>—All the people that opt in to your database, connect with you through Social Media, and are referred to you in some way. This can still be a very general and generic group of people.
3. <u>Discovery</u>—These people allow an interview process where questions are asked, ideas are presented, and there is an opportunity to agree that there is a basis for doing business together.
4. <u>Custom Proposal</u>—We put together a custom proposal when all parties agree that there is a basis for doing business together.
5. <u>Commitment</u>—This is where some objection handling or selling may need to take place in order to get the Suspect to commit to moving forward.

6. <u>Collect</u>—Even though people commit verbally or even in writing, it means nothing until the money is collected and continues to be collected!

7. <u>Start of Fulfillment</u>—Those first couple days and weeks are so important with a new client. Expectations are set, momentum is created, and credits are placed in the relationship bank. It is almost impossible to finish right when you start wrong.

8. <u>Completion of Collecting</u>—Proactive explaining, billing, status reports, and friendly reminders are paramount in collecting all money owed.

9. <u>Finish of Fulfillment</u>—This should happen on every project sold and promised. For on-going service agreements, this can happen at the end of every month of services completed.

This process and pipeline is not easy and is a constant work in progress. However, it always helps to know what perfect looks like and what you should be working towards.

Regardless, understanding this pipeline helps business leaders and Icons alike make really good decisions about where sales are weak, where the pipeline is leaking or breaking down, and where their focus needs to go. This awareness also presents opportunities for training for your team. You can more easily forecast future revenues and the bandwidth needed inside your organization using this pipeline method.

This is how it translates into my business:

- Maybe one out of 50 <u>Prospects</u> become <u>Suspects</u>.
- About one out of five <u>Suspects</u> have a <u>Discovery</u> Meeting/Call with me or a team member.
- Roughly two out of three <u>Discovery Calls</u> end with an agreement, which leads to a <u>Custom Proposal</u>.
- Maybe two out of three <u>Custom Proposals</u> result in a <u>Commitment</u>.
- Nine out of 10 <u>Commitments</u> result in the first <u>Collected</u>

payment.

- Everyone that pays goes into the <u>Fulfillment</u> funnel.
- In the last six months, four out of five clients have completed all their payments.
- In the last six months, two out of three clients that have paid 100% have been 100% <u>Fulfilled</u> on services purchased, with the difference being largely due to clients not giving us everything we need to complete projects.
- What if over the last six months most of my proposals have ranged from $10,000-$25,000 and my average payout was roughly $17,000?

So if I want to make $1,000,000 gross in my "Services" business, I know that I need:

1. 58 fully-paid <u>Clients</u> over the course of the year.
2. Based on the averages above, this would require 73 people to sign up, which means 82 people need to <u>Commit</u> to a <u>Custom Proposal</u>.
3. In order to get those 82 people I would need 125 <u>Custom Proposals</u> to be written.
4. We could expect those numbers from 189 <u>Discovery Calls</u>, which breaks down to 16 per month, or four per week.
5. Those calls would be gleaned from 945 <u>Suspects</u>, which breaks down to 79 per month, or 20 per week.
6. And finally, a pool of Suspects that big would require an even larger pool of 47,250 <u>Prospects</u> for the year, which breaks down to 3,937 per month, or 984 per week.

This is the same process I perfected while consulting Inc. 500 Infusionsoft, a software company that I helped take from $7 million to $14 million from 2008-2009. I've been perfecting it even more over the last year and even six months. I suppose I will always be looking to improve my understanding and implementation of my perfect pipeline process.

By knowing and understanding the lifetime value of my client, I also know exactly what I can afford to invest in advertising, loyalty programs, gifts, and extras for potential clients and clients alike.

For example:

- What is our cost per lead in every marketing scenario?
- What is our cost per client acquisition in every selling scenario?
- What is our cost per client project completion in every fulfillment scenario?

You can't let yourself get lost in these numbers. I am a pretty good estimator, so I have become disciplined in always having a rough idea of where I am in my business. You should do the same.

By the way, this is what a good business owner, president, or CEO understands, as well as how to make it all happen from the top to the bottom. That includes the vision of the company, too. The teller at the bank should know the goals and mission of the CEO. Easier said than done, I know.

If you wear all these hats, like most Icon Advisors, then this is all for you. Don't worry. It can be done.

If you are like most people, you feel a certain amount of stress when people use words like "sales" and "negotiations." On the other hand, if you are like most people who follow me online then you would probably have loved the Harvard Negotiation course I took about a decade ago. There are many aspects of that course that I have implemented into my life, like not having a "pie mentality," understanding different types of negotiation personalities and how to communicate with them accordingly, and how to overcome objections. But there is one key to successful negotiation that has always stuck with me more than anything else. That number one key is preparation. Harvard teaches and emphasizes that the more prepared negotiator almost always gets what they want.

Now that doesn't mean that the other parties negotiating won't get what they want. After all, we always want the "win-win" or even the "win-win-win." However, they say preparation will determine more than

www.FanFunnelMindMaps.com

90 percent of the outcome of any negotiation. Let's reverse engineer this preparation process step-by-step. Here is what I have learned as I have implemented Harvard's teachings into my own businesses and life:

1. First, you have to know what you want out of any given situation, deal, or potential agreement. There is nothing wrong with going on a fact-finding mission or doing a

discovery call, but even in these situations, you should know what success looks like in every communication. What you want to learn, what you want to understand, and what you want to communicate are fundamental elements in every encounter. When you don't know what you want from a meeting, you leave room for an ambush, to be caught off guard, to be posed questions you are not ready to answer, and to be in conversations you cannot intelligently maneuver. I regularly ask the leaders in my companies how they will define success before they go into meetings. It doesn't matter if they are doing an employee review, interviewing a potential employee, or choosing a vendor for a new service. My team must know what success looks like at the start of every meeting. This is step one.

2. Next, you must have a pretty good idea of what the other party or parties would like to accomplish. There is nothing wrong with finding that out in the meeting to some degree, but a prepared negotiator and communicator already has at least some idea. To have some creative solutions and options in advance is paramount in negotiating a successful outcome. Case studies, examples of what other people have done in your negotiating scenario, can also be very helpful. Almost every industry has standard ways they barter, discount, and creatively offer various options. Knowing these things will also make you more prepared.

3. Almost as important as the first two points is to understand the limits to what you can agree to and ultimately do. So not only do you want to define best case scenario (success), but you also want to define worst case scenario. For example, I learned after my first couple of car purchases that I needed to know exactly what I wanted to pay, exactly what I could afford in payments,

and exactly what kind of vehicle I wanted. Otherwise I was unprepared, and after a day at a dealership, I was making decisions that I later regretted. In those situations, I was the less-prepared party, and at least once I paid dearly for it. In the heat of the moment, when emotions are running high, it's only the prepared negotiator who will attain success.

4. Finally, try not to be the victim of your own negotiating success. There are many times that I could negotiate a better initial deal or an outcome for myself, but then you have to ask if that's what's best in the long run. Taking advantage of people, creating extremely lop sided deals, and pulling fast ones will almost always come back to bite you. Ethics aside, it is just bad business to burn bridges and create a bad name for yourself. Sometimes you will have to look out for the other party because they are not as prepared as you. Sometimes you will have to think ahead and prepare for their best outcome too. If you can do this, then you are almost guaranteed ongoing successful negotiations in the future which will prepare you for the next encounter with that party.

These four things will put all the odds in your favor for more successful communications and negotiations. I hope you want nothing but the best for those around you as well as yourself, and I hope you get everything you want in your next negotiation. Just be careful what you negotiate for because you will most likely get it!

Chapter 29

Prospects and Suspects

Prospects

A prospect can be just about anyone. Don't get me wrong; we always want to be prospecting and mining in the best places possible. However, we have to accept that this is the top of the funnel and the very start of the pipeline. To judge too harshly too early by eliminating people from your pool of prospects could mean lost opportunities.

You need to think in terms of "impressions" in this phase of the process. Impressions are all about exposure. Every time someone hears your radio commercial, sees you on a billboard as they drive by, hears your name in a conversation, or even scrolls past your most recent post on Facebook—that is an impression.

Prospects come from and through impressions. Now might be a good time to think about what you are doing to create impressions through people, places, and things. Good marketing, smart advertising, and happy clients are some of the best ways to create good numbers of healthy impressions.

Suspects

This category is made of people who do very suspicious things and take suspicious actions. You see, even before a potential client enters the formal sales process, we should be familiar with what they do. Knowing these habits help us better recognize and communicate with our leads.

You need to think in terms of "introductions" when it comes to this phase in the process. The key to introductions is action. This is when people not only see your number, but decide to call it. This is when people not just see your website, but decide to visit it. This is when people see your video image, and actually decide to view it.

In terms of online marketing, this is where they read, click, view, comment, or share your information with others. By taking any of these actions, people can go from being Prospects to Suspects. They may even be guilty of wanting to get prices or even talk business very soon.

The more you can interact with people live, in real time or through automation, the better. Inter action has never been more valuable than at this point in history.

At one time, marketing and advertising were sent off into the atmosphere as a one-way message, never to be heard from again. Nowadays it's different.

People want dialogue, and they want to ask follow-up questions. Icons that can respond intelligently in a decent amount of time will always have the advantage. Regardless of any Icon status, people want authenticity and two-way communication. They do not want to work with rich people living in ivory towers who think they are too important to interact with the world.

Now might be a good time to think about what you are doing to create more introductions through sharing valuable content and ideas. Good marketing, smart advertising, and happy clients are some of the best ways to create good numbers of healthy introductions.

Chapter 30

Where 91% of my Business Comes From

As I shared with you earlier, I use social media, email marketing, books, and events to generate virtually all my business, but did you know that over 90 percent of those contacts, readers, and event attendees are referred to me by someone else?

That's right, referral partners make up 91 percent of my business.

You probably get your best leads from referrals too, but do you actually have a referral reward system or an affiliate program that pays out commissions? You should.

Here are seven ways I attract leads from influencers in the industry.

1. On a white board, write out ten to twenty names of the people you know who you want to work with. I want the daily visual reminder of the people I regularly need to communicate with. My team has meetings where we discuss our referral partners by name and how the relationship is going.

2. Pick up the phone to call these people and meet with them face to face. Short, effective calls and meetings with a purpose can be very powerful. Longer hang outs from time to time can be valuable too. Texting is also a

3. surprisingly effective way to stay on someone's mind and be efficient with everyone's time. Just avoid text letters.

4. Have multiple ways to reward your relationships. Referral commissions are just one way to reward those people sending you business. I'm always thinking about ways to give, serve, and share with my strategic partners. Maybe it's celebrating them online or introducing them to my contacts or providing a service at a discounted rate.

5. Make it easy for people to refer you! Give your referral partners what to say, what to show, and the best ways to refer you. Give them testimonial video links, website URLs, media kits, and examples of your work. Teach them how to introduce you, what a good lead is for you, and what a bad lead is for you. Make it easy for them!

6. Take care of the referrals you get from your strategic referral partners. This can be tough at times, but you have to take care of these people. The worst thing that can happen to a referral relationship is to have to apologize for introducing someone to someone else.

7. Don't let referral partners get random. High-profit, low-maintenance referral partnerships don't happen by accident. They take work and almost constant over communication. I consciously think about and work on my referral partnerships. I make time to make the calls, ask the questions, serve the people, and reward the referrals! You must be consciously consistent when it comes to this instrumental area of your business.

8. Go deep! You have to know your referral partners' goals, ambitions, and reasons for living. How do they define success? What makes them tick? What are the easy and hard wins that are worth it? Be thoughtful and follow up about business and life.

Yes, I have funnels. Yes, I market online. Yes, I write books. Yes, I put on events. Yes, I speak often on TV. But it's relationships that feed these funnels, fill my databases, share my materials, and invite people to meet me. Do you have enough referral partners? Do you have enough of the right kind of referral partners? Are you rewarding your referral partners enough? Is it a process that is predictable and on purpose? If not, maybe it's time to review and refocus.

Grow your referral relationships deep and wide, and everything else will start to happen a little more automatically—guaranteed.

Chapter 31

Discovery Calls Make the Connection

Discovery Calls should be very innocent and scheduled with no presumptuous overtones. The only purpose here is to sincerely enter into a very relationship-focused conversation with very few motives other than finding out if the two of you could work together.

You need to think in terms of "connections" when it comes to this phase of the process. The key to connections is permission. Discovery calls only happen once you have made a connection and have received permission to communicate with the person.

These kinds of connections happen when people give you their card, opt in on your website, or leave their phone number on your voice mail or with your team. They also happen when someone friends you on Facebook, subscribes to you on YouTube, connects with you on LinkedIn, or follows you on Twitter.

In all these cases, these people have now given you permission to communicate with them. This is how Discovery Call possibilities are born. And even though there is now a possibility, it is still up to you to schedule the call and make it happen.

It should be done at a time and in an environment that will have the least distractions. Noisy restaurants, their office, their home, and other places where there's a high risk for interruptions should all be avoided.

In addition, they should have been sent materials to review and absorb before the meeting. Examples of your work, various testimonials, awards, and endorsements should all be sent in advance. Experts and Icons have these kinds of things built, prepared, and ready to be deployed at any time.

There is probably no better interview process than a High Trust Interview, which you can learn in detail by reading Todd Duncan's book *High Trust Selling*. Even if you do his process halfway wrong, you will probably still make twice as much.

Bottom line: You need to find out what drives these people as a person and as a professional. You need to know both their personal goals as well as their business goals.

> You need to find out what drives people, both personally and professionally.

Ease their pain

In order for people to get better results, they have to change what they are currently doing.

Unfortunately, change generally happens only once someone regularly experiences enough pain. You would think more people would be motivated by the carrot, but the most action is taken because of the proverbial stick.

For years I preferred, and even targeted, people who met two criteria:

1. They had money.
2. They had a proven way to make more money.

I could expand on this, but these simple bullets are good for anyone in the advice business to follow. Plus, the more money they have and the more money they can make, the better your odds are for making the most for your advice...or at least so I thought.

It turns out there are a few other bullets worth considering, with one in particular being the biggest bullet by far:

It's PAIN! The prospective client needs to have pain. The more pain, the better, and although I don't relish the fact that people are in pain, I acknowledge that these are my clients to some degree.

ER doctors don't hope for more patients, paramedics aren't praying for more 911 calls, and I don't hope for more struggling businesses. Yet those are the people I have been called to help, and I love strengthening businesses!

I have worked with some big names and organizations, but the hardest sales are the ones where the prospective client just doesn't have a lot of pain. It's amazing how much agony people can live with and ultimately get used to.

Sometimes it's our job as trusted advisors to help point out the pain they have grown accustomed to during the Discovery Call session.

A lot of time can be wasted pursuing affluent people who don't have pain or won't acknowledge their agony. A lot can be done through automated follow up, but when it comes to your personal time, ask yourself if the Prospect/Suspect meets the following criteria:

1. They have money.
2. They have a proven way to make more money.
3. They have pain!

The people ready to take the most action are those who meet all of the above criteria. Anything less could still be considered a warm lead, but make sure you are prioritizing correctly. Otherwise, you'll be the one experiencing more pain.

A good discovery call will consist of you asking strategic questions that help to identify the areas of pain, listening to the answers, and then providing stimulating ideas and solutions to the problems. These ideas should be relevant, quantifiable, preferably come with examples of how you have done it for others, and present an "under promise, over deliver" opportunity.

This means you should not have to promise the moon or unrealistic results to get and keep the Suspect's attention. The more powerful the marketing collateral you sent prior to the discovery call, the less you will need to over promise. The greater the Icon status, the less you will need to over promise. Your reputation of results should speak for itself.

Now might be a good time to revisit your Icon status. Are you capturing and creating the social proof you need to own every room you ever enter? No matter what you already have, you will need more. Never stop documenting your success, collecting testimonials, and recruiting endorsements. Winning an award every once in a while isn't bad either.

Pick up the freaking phone

Maybe I should just smile as the excuses flood the streets about why there are no sales. Sales and marketing people have been lulled into the soothing light of the computer screen. Business people in general are suffering from serious call reluctance—but sometimes you just have to pick up the freaking phone and actually call someone!

Yes, Facebook can be effective; LinkedIn has its place, and double yes—everyone is loving video. But appointment or not, we all need to physically "reach out and touch someone" a little more often. I, too, am guilty of this from time to time, and it always shocks me how much farther and faster things go when I just actually talk to someone.

Here are a couple of tips to leverage that "Old School" sales tool called the phone:

1. First ask if you caught them at a good time.
2. Be brief and be conscious of people's time.
3. Be personal, but get to the point.
4. Make sure you have a take away or a next step before you get off the phone.

Now, if you are finding this difficult, then you are probably just hiding out, scared of potential rejection. This is NOT good. Some of the following might be your problem(s):

1. You don't know your product/service.
2. You don't know what people may ask you.
3. You don't know how to handle objections.
4. You don't know how to relate to and build rapport with people.

Notice that all of these are about "knowing" something. Friend, there are no new objections in the world, and you have to believe in what you are selling. That's right. I used that bad word "sales." We all need others to take action, whether money is exchanging hands or not, and that's okay! Learn to be good with people. It's your job, whether you realize it or not.

Foreplay doesn't make a baby, and you can quote me on that. I see so much teasing and playing around out there that goes nowhere. I know it's a numbers game, but I promise conversions will improve by picking up the freaking phone.

This is a lost art that, if harnessed, will help you kill the competition. The funny thing is that the people you talk to every once in a while are the ones who will actually respond the most to your emails and social media. Go call someone now before you lose any more business.

Focus on a solution for them, a win for you

These calls should end with clear next steps. You should have all the information you need to write up a custom proposal.

Asking to take notes, taking notes, and using those notes when creating your proposal are imperative. Focus your notes on the things that they have the most energy about and the things that are the easiest wins for you.

These calls should typically end after thirty to sixty minutes. A person should never be rushed at this point in the process, but there must be a beginning and an end. After all, you are a professional and a highly sought-after Icon.

If you are an influential Icon, then you should also leave them with more information and content to review. You can even give them names of people that you have worked with in the past so that they might contact them for more verification of your success and accomplishments. This whole Discovery Process is where any Icon will crush the competition by being prepared and practiced with social proof.

Chapter 32

Custom Proposals

Now that you've remembered that picking up the freaking phone actually still works as a business tool, it's time to turn to another too, the custom proposal.

These proposals aren't a literary tap dance; they should be very simple and easy to read. They also should not be confused with contracts. There are different rules, regulations, and laws from industry to industry, all of which need to be followed to the fullest.

You need to think in terms of an audience when you think of these proposals. The key to audiences is that you have to get both action and permission from the Suspects. If done right, you will have earned this right to share your thoughts, ideas, and proposals to an individual decision maker.

Notice I said decision maker. We never want to write proposals to anyone less than a decision maker. The person receiving the proposal must have the right and control of the money to make the decision.

Every proposal must have these components:

Prices

1. Discounts
2. Numbered and bulleted, segmented categories of thought.
3. Options that are simple and clear.
4. Examples or references of how you have successfully done what

you are proposing for other people.
5. A clear break down of what your products and services entail.
6. Projections of any potential results.

This is equally an art and a science. Writing proposals is just as important as verbally over coming objections and getting people to take action. It is generally perfected over time, just like anything else.

Over time you will discover that you can use past proposals when writing new ones. Or at least you can repurpose some of the same structure, verbiage, and successful examples of how you have done work for others.

You should also refrain from using social media messages to convey proposals. Emails have a better emotional trigger and business feel to them. Simply put, they are just more professional.

Prices

Whether it's "Sales Psychology" or "Average Individual Economics," there are price points and price breaks that can be followed to maximize profits. Here are a few factors to consider when pricing your products and services:

1. What does the competition charge?
2. What kind of ROI can you provide for a customer?
3. What kind of experience can you provide for a customer?

None of these questions will give you a definitive answer to this complex question, but they will put all the odds in your favor when it comes to configuring the best price structure. So let's go a little deeper and talk about numbers.

Here are some numbers that we have tested in dozens of industries over years of marketing.

1. Someone who pays $1 won't necessarily pay more.
2. Someone who pays $2 will probably pay $5, but someone who pays $5 won't necessarily pay more.

3. Someone who pays $6 will probably pay $7, $8, or even $9; but someone who pays $9 won't necessarily pay $10 or more.
4. Someone who pays $10 will generally spend all the way up to $19.
5. Someone who pays $20 will pay up to $27 or even $29.
6. Someone who pays $30 will generally pay all the way up $59.
7. Someone who pays $60 will generally pay all the way up to $99.

Here are some current sexy numbers that have been shown to trigger purchases, but this could change if the market sees too much of them:

$1

$2

$5

$7

$9

$17

$27

$59

$97

$197, $297, $397, $497, $597, $697, $797, $897

$997

$1497

$1997

$2497

$2997

$3497

$3997

$4997

You probably notice a pattern here. Interestingly enough, I have found that someone who can afford and will pay $6,000 for something will also pay $7,497 or even $9,997. Of course, there is a real break and a big difference between $6,000-$9000 and that $10,000 plus mark. In addition, once you get into the thousands, people can talk about and review numbers when they are listed out with a "k." For example:

- 3k is better than $3,000
- 4k is better than $4,000
- 5k is better than $5,000 and so on

Another key to predicting the right price point is to make it a number that doesn't stand out. We've tried to mix it up several times with $8 or $88, but people just think too much about it, no matter how cool it looks.

You can charge more in person versus online, too. People typically don't want to pay thousands of dollars online on a credit card without talking to someone. If you create a funnel where people baby step with smaller price points and develop a relationship, then they are more likely to spend the bigger dollar amounts without a call or a face-to-face.

Start looking at what you charge and see if you need to change price points. I've made people a lot of money by increasing the highest break.

Discounts

There is an expression that goes something like this: "A confused buyer is not a buyer." Simply put, stop confusing people. Now more than ever, our proposals, offers, and promotions need to make sense. They need to pass the smell test.

Have you have seen a promotional package that is usually sold for $25,000 and is now $1? Or how about the "I have only four products left" scarcity tactic? Who do they think they are fooling? Who actually believes that? No one I know, that's for sure.

Now, I know I am going to take some real heat for saying all this. My speaker and marketer friends are going to be sending me some nasty emails for sure. I may have even lost a few.

> *My* speaker friends are going to be sending me some nasty emails for sure.

But even if those tactics are using true data (there is such a thing as really good deals on products that once sold for more money, and true, sincere scarcity), things nowadays need to really make sense. This is called Make Sense Marketing, and you must enter the "NO HYPE ZONE."

The fact that we must tell the truth is a given, but are we also making sure our marketing message is one that makes sense? Here are some examples of how I use Make Sense Marketing in my business:

1. I might put on a free event, but I always explain I am recording the event so that I can have video to sell and use for future marketing. The fact that I am getting something out of the event makes them feel less skeptical about my motives. I will even say something like, "Now before you think I am a really nice guy, let me explain why this event is free."

2. I might give pretty big discounts after the first one or two projects I do for a client, but I always explain that once I know more about a client's business or objectives, the next projects are much easier. Notice that it's not only the truth, but it makes sense.

3. I might not have a limited number of packages to sell, but I tell people that I do have a limited amount of time. When my calendar fills up, it fills up. I explain that if they want to get going, then they should move fast. I also explain that we are always finishing projects, so the worst-case scenario is that it might be a month or two before I am able to bring on a new project. So yes, there is a sense of urgency, but there is not an insincere scarcity scare.

Look at all your marketing. Think about what you are saying and review your proposals and offers because they need to make sense. Your ideas and communication must be congruent with what people are seeing in the world. It's not enough to just be truthful or authentic. Make sure you make sense. This is Make Sense Marketing. Remember, a confused buyer is NOT a buyer.

Clarity

Everything has the need to be quick, easy to absorb, and succinct. Benjamin Franklin's quote that proves truer today than ever is, "If I had more time, I would have written a shorter letter."

Everyone is busy, but decision makers seem even more prone to be hurting for time because everyone is coming to them for decisions. In addition, the typical decision maker seems to have ADHD. Of course, it may just be that the whole world's attention span has changed.

Instead of traditional movies, there's growing demand for short films. Twenty-two minute TV episodes are losing market share to six- to nine-minute webisodes. Social media platforms often require us to limit our message to as little as 200 characters, and 140 if you're on Twitter.

It does, in fact, take more time to successfully communicate clearly with fewer words—and even characters for that matter. Yet great proposals do just that. You just don't have the luxury of expecting people to read long email proposals. Of course, the greater the Icon status, the more time, attention, and reading you can expect.

I don't care whether or not you like Barack Obama. If you got a letter from him, you would read every word twice.

Other than the length, I write my proposals in a similar format to the way I'm writing this book, with lots of bullets, numbers, and fast-paced segments. It must have the feeling of going smoothly, being easy to read, and even easier to skim.

Your custom proposal should start with a recap of previous

conversations, then explain where the client is now, where he or she wants to go, and what it will take to get there. Use numbers and bullets.

Then show the value of what you offer, followed by the price and any discounts that apply. Just make sure that the discounts make sense. The same applies to projections. You need to have them, but they better be safe and make sense.

Prospective clients always want to know the return on their investment. They want to know what does the before and after look like? What results are typical? What results are possible, even if not typical?

Other questions for various industries might

1. How much healthier can I be?
2. How much will I learn?
3. How much money will I make?
4. How fast will I learn?
5. How fast can I get results?
6. How much better will I look?
7. How much better will I feel?
8. How much time will this save me?
9. How many more leads will I get?
10. How fast can I get it done?

Come up with safe answers that are deeply rooted in past experiences with clients. As I said before, you should under promise and over deliver every time. Even if you aren't necessarily aiming for under promising, be sure that over delivering is always the consistent outcome.

And remember, people don't buy the process; they buy the result. Focus on the results in the proposal. Explain the process, but only as part of the result and what it means to reach that result.

End with links to testimonials, websites, and examples of things that prove you are the best person for the job. The proposal should have the feeling that you have earned the right to propose and that you are working to earn their business. Nothing is taken for granted.

Chapter 33

3 Steps to Commitment

Getting a commitment from the prospective client may still be one of the hardest things to do in the pipeline process, but it's relatively easy for people with an Icon status. This is where all your influence, credibility, and exposure should pay off.

When the proposal is met with a yes, this chapter will seem sort of worthless. When the proposal is met with rejection or indecision, this chapter becomes one of the most empowering ones you will ever read.

Other than determining the objections and working to overcome them in a non-adversarial role, you need to just work on three things.

The first thing you want to do is work on the relationship. People typically do business with people they like, admire, respect, and trust. You need to sincerely take an interest in that person and make sure you can relate and connect with them.

There is an expression that people don't care how much you know until they know how much you care. So do you care? Do they know you care?

Next is the question of value. If people who trust you have the money and know the value of what you offer, you are doing just about everything you can to win the business.

The more examples, testimonials, and details you can provide about the value the better. The book How to Win Friends and Influence

People, by Dale Carnegie, is a must read for any Icon. The same can be said for 25 Ways to Win with People, by my favorite self-improvement author John C. Maxwell.

My personal style is to give people time and space and then to strategically follow up. Follow up is so key and it is where so many businesses fall short.

I know that timing is everything, so we never want to start over with just new leads every month. Rather, we want to continue to follow up on past proposals so that when they are ready, they think of us first and foremost.

So many good prospects and Suspects fall through the cracks and go to the competition just because there is no follow up. Todd Duncan taught me a powerful lesson, which I always pass on to businesses with a series of telling questions: Have you been in business five years, or one year five times? Or have you been in business for one year, or one month twelve times? What I'm really asking here is are you constantly starting over, or is your marketing reaching critical mass and multiplying? If you aren't sure, start getting serious about going for the commitment. Remember the big 3: Relationship, Value, and Follow up.

Chapter 34

5 Authentic
Negotiation Best Practices

The problem with most negotiation tactics and practices is they can feel phony or as if you are playing games. Instead of embellishing or exaggerating situations and circumstances, you want to actually create them and share them in real life. Some of the best advice I ever got was from a billionaire who told me everything changed for him when he had "go to hell money"...his words not mine.

Let me explain with 5 Authentic Negotiation Best Practices:

1. There is a lot of power in having options. Busy people get better offers. This means you need to actually be busy and work on always having lots of possibilities. So much of negotiation is who needs who more and who can afford to walk away the easiest, so stay moving. We negotiate better when we have a busy business. Sometimes I do things for less money just to get busy; once busy, I can always charge more or get my real value. It's how to command by being in demand.

2. People need to know just how busy and productive you really are. Again, this can't be a game you play. You need to really be busy, anxiously engaged in a good cause. Be visibly involved in valuable activities. Testimonials, endorsements, before and after pictures, and awards are

just a few of the ways you can share the proof of your productivity.

3. Be unreachable or inaccessible because you are so busy. Everyone, especially entrepreneurs, are starting things all the time. It's extremely more effective to show people you are accomplishing your goals and finishing meaningful metrics in your world. Don't always attend the same events, don't always go to the same places, and make sure you are making the rounds.

4. You can't be in a hurry or too presumptuous. If you want to go faster than everyone else, you may give up some of your value to make things move more quickly. Once busy with a certain percentage of your time, then you can afford to play it cool...because you are cool! Rushing the relationship is one of the top mistakes people make in the business world today.

5. Explain your schedule, client load, priorities, and projects. Things should connect and add up. I call this 'make sense marketing'. Things need to make sense. People need things to pass the smell test. They can sniff out confusion pretty easily, and a confused buyer isn't a buyer. Your prices, products, and programs should make sense. People understand successful people are productively busy.

So actually be busy, let the world know how busy, be unreachable to a certain degree, be in demand, don't be in a hurry, and make sure things make sense. People want to work with high achievers and celebrity experts, and they understand successful people are productively busy.

I once asked a billionaire, Paul B., about when everything really changed for him or when things came together. His answer was when he got "go to hell money". Of course I was very curious and just stared at him with a smile. He explained once he had enough money and profitable projects that he could tell people to go to hell when he didn't want to work on something or with someone, everything changed for him. Once he could really pick and choose how he spent his time, he could really just pick the best of everything. You see, once he was at this point people needed him more than he needed them.

Now, you might not like his choice of words or you may not even like this attitude, but I sure hope you get the negotiation power of being busy, having some money, and knowing how to leverage both accordingly. Sure, in the beginning you may need to discount, wheel and deal, and work on earning some experience, but eventually you should breaking through to the other side.

Chapter 35

Collect

Even though this is a short chapter, it's a big principle. A sale is never done and a new relationship with a client is never started without payment. Remember, there are a lot of things competing for the war chest, and people's priorities are changing daily, if not hourly.

I love checks, but I hate the mail. You may want to choose having a Fed Ex account as I do. Regular mail embodies somewhat of a mystery when it comes to travel time. Fed Ex or mail with a tracking number is solid. As soon as someone commits to the proposal, I send an invoice and mailing instructions with my Fed Ex account number. Then I track the money all the way to my hand. It's worth the money to know it's officially done.

Of course face-to-face meetings make this process pointless, but it is the way to go. Credit cards and merchant banking are nice to have but meaningless when it comes to bigger amounts. Not to mention, the fees can be high.

Either way, it's important to realize it's not done until there is money cleared in your account, so you need to proceed accordingly until it is done-done.

I'm not a pest, and I am always professional, but I have actually gone to the bank with new clients to collect the money. No money, no sale. Take it to heart, because getting paid for what you do is the heart of your business.

All the Money

Collecting money is one of the hardest things a company has to do. Icons especially hate it and are sometimes bad at it because they feel they are too good to ask for their money.

You have to collect, or you have to empower someone else to collect. Either way, ignoring this aspect of your business will cause you to not only lose some of your Icon status, but to lose money.

You need happy, successful clients who have finished your process and experienced your rewarding results. There will be times when this just isn't possible, so having a collections policy is good business. You can take payments, barter, sue, and even forgive debts. Whatever you choose, just do something. You can't let these matters go unattended. They foster resentment, and resentment can ignite feelings of revenge.

There are people who owe me money and have owed me money for some time. I have owed people money as well. This is just a part of business that has to be met head on. If people don't pay you, then you can't pay others. I've been there before, too. If you are going to net six figures and more, you have to proactively work with people to collect the money you have agreed to.

These matters should be private, respectful, and solution-focused. Let people vent and explain as you actively listen, but then move the conversation toward solutions.

Chapter 36

Making Business a Relationship

You hope to be doing business with your new client for some time; you hope to obtain referrals from this person down the road. Now that you have the account is just the beginning of many ways you can continue to stand out.

Those first couple of days and weeks are so important with a new client. Expectations are set, momentum is created, and credits are placed in the relationship bank. It is almost impossible to finish right when you start wrong.

Welcome calls, welcome packets, and proactive checklists are all of huge value. I am also a firm believer in the "Easy Win." In every business, I have always found an easy win for an Icon Advisor to execute in the first couple of days. This entails finding some small, yet significant task that you can accomplish for the new client.

- If you will be shooting pictures and video, send a checklist with good ideas of what to wear for the upcoming shoot.
- If you are a Realtor, put together a quick list of homes that meet the clients' criteria.
- If you are a publisher, get them a couple mockup example covers to look at and get their wheels turning.
- Some attorneys are sending out videos to watch so that they might be more prepared for the first appointment.
- Some optometrists have apps that allow you to take a picture

of yourself and put various glasses on your picture digitally so that you can see how you would look with specific frames.

- If you are an architect, send your new client the top ten house plans of the year before.
- If you are chiropractor, send your new client some vitamins that best fit their anticipated needs.

All these actions help you obtain positive momentum. This, combined with proactive execution, is almost unstoppable. Over the years, my greatest desire has been to learn people's needs and discover ways to anticipate them more regularly.

Clients never like looking for you or tracking you down for progress updates. You should pretty quickly be able to figure out the information your clients will want to know. The next step is to set up a proactive report that goes out to them electronically as well as over the phone. The more control you have over your time, the better you'll be able to stay on top of these important connections.

We need to reduce the number of interruptions we have over the course of a day. Ask yourself, do you run your day, or does your day run you? Do you control your email, your social media, and your phone or do they control you? The more proactive your reporting systems, the less you are reacting out of control during the day.

Celebrating people is the ultimate introduction!

If you're like me, then you attend a lot of events and do a fair amount of networking online.

You have a very awesome opportunity at quality events to meet with successful people and form new profitable relationships. The same opportunity applies online in the right social media groups, hangouts, and meetups. You have the chance to make a great first impression...IF you get a brilliant introduction. You see, the best connectors, promoters, and networkers know how to celebrate people and their accomplishments in an introduction.

Everyone knows how much I practice and preach social proof. This is the ability to have third-party endorsements, support, and praise blazing your marketing trail. Every time I introduce someone, it includes not only their name, but a small list of impressive accomplishments that are most relevant to that person or the audience that I am introducing them to.

This may sound simple, but it is an art worth perfecting.

The introduction style I have is not one filled with hype or embellishments; rather it's sincere and from the heart in my own unique way and with my own words. I summarize, highlight, and connect the dots for everyone to see the great and unique nature of the people I introduce. Sometimes I don't always have the time to do the introduction justice, but it's always my goal to celebrate people with a sincere, sophisticated style.

I focus on a couple of talking categories like Icon accomplishments and humanitarian efforts. This includes what they have published, media they have been featured on, awards they have won, schools they have attended, degrees they have earned, stages they have spoken on, celebrities who have endorsed them, famous associations that they have, boards they sit on, charities they support, families they have, and especially all the kind things that they have done for me. When you celebrate people, they want to be around you more. They want to attend your events, visit your office, and contribute to your conversations online and in social media. When you celebrate people, they want to celebrate you!

Although I have enjoyed the moniker of the Icon Builder, the moniker of Celebration Artist would be just as flattering to me. When we promote less and celebrate more, everyone wins.

Chapter 37

The Finish Lines

Yes, there is more than one finish line for all Icon Advisors, and some have more finish lines than others. There is being done; there is getting feedback, revisions, improving things. And then there is being done-done.

When you have an ongoing monthly process or service, "done" also looks a little different. No matter what service or product you offer, there needs to be a definition of what "done" is. Everyone both internally in your organization and externally outside your organization needs to understand what that definition is.

Finishing fulfillment of products and services, and finishing collections of the money can be very elusive. Clients not getting you what you need, vacillating ideas, evolution of ideas, and too many cooks in the kitchen can have a huge impact on whether or not you reach the finish line in a timely manner, or at all.

Constant, clear, proactive communication is the best way to handle these things. And over time, you will learn that there will always be warning signs.

Once you start reaching some of the various finish lines, you should be asking for testimonials, both written and video, on the things that are done and done well.

You do not have to be done with every aspect of a transaction to have earned the right to ask for and receive a testimonial. The best thing to do is to create an environment for gratitude and compliments.

Every testimonial can be considered one of your finish lines. The last finish line is when all the work is done, everyone is paid, and everyone is happy.

The most common definitions of happiness are...

1. Good fortune
2. Prosperity
3. A state of well-being and contentment
4. A pleasurable or satisfying experience

My new definition of happiness comes from being an entrepreneur, an "idea guy," a person who loves to create and start new things. My new definition of happiness can be summed up in one word... "FINISHING." Happiness is finishing. For me it's that simple.

Successful people are finishers. What have you started that you need to finish?

If you can figure that out and prioritize things correctly, you have some guaranteed happiness coming your way. I think I figured this out a few years ago when I came up with hiring someone to be my "Finisher." This person's job was to do nothing but help me finish all the things I started. For a while, they even had the email finisher@davidtfagan.com." (Maybe I should have them use that again.)

The truth is, I have several people these days dedicated to helping me finish more projects in my life. Happiness has come from finishing:

1. Books
2. Events
3. Acquiring organizations
4. Hiring the right people
5. Websites

What would make you the most money and mean the most to your business if you could finish it in the next thirty days? What do you want, and what are you willing to give up to get it?

We have only so much time. This means that as busy people, in order for something new in our life to live, something old must die. Have you killed the right time-consuming activities and projects in your life? Before you start anything new, you must realize that real happiness may come from finishing something else first.

My friend and associate Roger Salam talks about Project Pruning exercises. Here's what he would tell you.

1. Make a list of all your projects.
2. Create columns for the potential profitability of the project, the time it might take, and how much you might actually enjoy that particular project.
3. Then start analyzing the information to find the easy wins with most profits in the shortest time that you like doing the most.

A lot can go into this exercise, but I've found this process to be very helpful. Of course, as you start various projects and activities, new information may come in that may change the priority or importance of those "to do's", so feel free to change directions as needed.

Bottom line: starting less and finishing more will lead to greater happiness in your life.

Chapter 38

Reverse Engineering

Start with these questions. If you want to be really serious, get a piece of paper and something to write with.

1. How much money do you want to make over the next years?
2. How much do you gross, or how much do you net on every sale?
3. Divide number 1 by number 2 and that's how many sales you need. Just remember that not every sale turns into a fully paid sale or client.
4. How many sales do you need to close in order to come up with the requisite number of fully-paid sales? Does every one you sign up or sell pay all the way through? What is the percentage of people who do? Maybe you need to sign up and sell more people because some don't pay all the way through, or at all.
5. How many proposals do you have to submit to get the necessary number of committed sales calculated in number 4?
6. How many discovery calls does it take to generate the number of proposals in number 5? What does that break down to per month, week, or day?
7. How many suspects does it take to materialize into the necessary number of discovery calls in number 6? What does that break down to per month, week, or day?
8. How many people do you need in your pool of prospects for

the year to generate the necessary number of suspects calculated in number 7? What does that break down to per month, or week? Re member, prospects are all the people who have been exposed to you and your organization.

Chapter 39

Direct Dollars

Now that you know the numbers of the "Pipeline with a Purpose," you need to work on what will feed the funnel of Prospects, Suspects, Discovery calls, and Custom Proposals. Now the questions are:

1. What marketing activities will get me Prospects, Suspects, and Discovery calls?

2. What advertising activities will get me Prospects, Suspects, and Discovery calls?

3. What strategic partners will refer me Prospects, Suspects, and Discovery calls?

If you need sixteen discovery calls every week, how many of those calls can you rely on yourself to generate? Who else can you enlist to refer you to others and help generate calls? How many can each of those people be counted on to generate? Every relationship needs an estimated value in this way. Ask yourself, do you have eight people who can set up two discovery calls for you? Maybe you have only four people who can refer two, and so you still need to account for eight more calls.

Maybe you run an ad on the radio station that will give you four more discovery calls. Maybe you market yourself on Facebook, and that will give you four more calls. Maybe you speak once a month at various local events, and this always provides two discovery calls. Maybe you are able to sell right from the stage, and that gives you two actual clients.

A direct-dollar activity is all about fulfilling the numbers in the pipeline formula. What's most important is to know where the numbers are coming from, protect those sources, reward those sources, and value those activities. So many Icon Advisors could do more with fewer sources if they just really protected and rewarded them.

Direct-Dollar activities include:

1. Speaking in public.
2. Working with social media.
3. Attending networking events.
4. Making potential affiliates or referrers of business fans by giving, serving, and sharing with them.
5. Getting strategic partners to talk about you, email about you, and create posts about you in social media.
6. Make clients fans and work with them to help them refer you business.
7. Advertise in trade publications, radio, billboards, etc.

There are other industry-specific direct-dollar activities that you need to learn about. Realtors can do open houses, fitness trainers can offer a free session(s) to help people experience the process, and speakers can put on free or affordable events where people can come hear what they are all about.

You will also come to realize that some activities will be high dollar and some will be low dollar. In the beginning, low-dollar activities are better than no-dollar activities. Actually, any activity is better than no activity.

You are not going to hit your dollar goals unless you can fill in the blank on where these leads for the pipeline are going to come from. Even then, you have to work those activities day in and day out.

It really just comes down to how you spend your time, and since we all have the same amount, you have to wonder why some people are more successful than others. The answer is coming.

Chapter 40

Cost Per

Once you understand the value of your clients in terms of dollars, you can really do a lot. More specifically, you can decide what you can afford to do to acquire more clients.

What if you knew that running a particular ad would get you…

1. 10,000 Impressions, which would turn into
2. 300 Introductions, which would turn into
3. 100 Connections, which would turn into
4. An audience of 33, which would most likely turn into
5. 3 Sales?

If you were then told the ad would cost you $1,000, you would know that breaks down to:

1. $.10 per impression.
2. $3.33 per introduction.
3. $10 per connection.
4. $33.30 per audience member (discovery call)

Fans by the #'s & $'s

$1,000

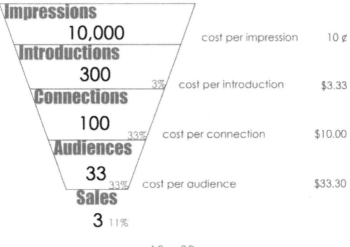

Impressions 10,000	cost per impression	10 ¢
Introductions 300 3%	cost per introduction	$3.33
Connections 100 33%	cost per connection	$10.00
Audiences 33 33%	cost per audience	$33.30
Sales 3 11%		

10 = 30
100 = 300
1,000 = 3,000
10,000 = 30,000

Now the questions become, "What are you selling and how much are you making?" Based off those conversion numbers and costs, you couldn't afford to run that ad if you sold something for $300. But it totally makes sense if you make $3,000 per sale.

So what if the direct-dollar activity doesn't cost you anything?

Then all you need to do is to find out the true value of your time. The higher the hourly rate, the more important it is that you are doing the highest valued direct-dollar activities.

Now, that you're learning about the tools that can help you, I'm going to share the price of mistakes I hope you never make.

Fan Follow-up

Impressions
Introductions
Connections
Audiences
Sales

People don't buy when you're ready to sell.

Your most automation goes here.

January   February   March   April
3   +1   +1   +1

Chapter 41

2 Mistakes That Could Ruin You

In 2007, I lost a great deal of money, and I shocked myself right into reality. Business had always been easy for me. What had gone wrong? What I had and what I lost doesn't really matter now in hindsight. What matters most is what I learned, and what you can learn from my close call. I learned the hard way, and now I am going to share with you how to avoid two very simple mistakes.

1. The first is the myth that things pay for themselves. The idea that a copier, a nice car, nice clothes, etc. are all investments that will pay for themselves if done right is ridiculous. That everything is or can be some kind of an investment is totally bogus. Actually, most things can NOT be thought of this way. This is how rookie business owners (as I was in 2007) rationalize things they want to spend money on.

   We need to look at the cheapest, most affordable ways to purchase tools, office space, tech, furniture or equipment when growing our businesses. Most of these are just the cost of doing business, and they won't necessarily make you money just because you have them.

2. Then there is the myth that our time is all so valuable we should delegate all these lesser job duties and tasks. Like all the best lies that are told or that we tell ourselves, there has to be a certain amount of truth that is the trick to

selling the rest of the lie. In the beginning, our time just isn't worth all that much. We do need to do a lot of things ourselves until we can prove our time is valuable. For example, if you made $2,000 closing a deal in an hour some inexperienced idiot (like I was) could say that they make $2,000 an hour, yet that might be the only deal they close all month. And as I mentioned earlier, that same inexperienced idiot will no doubt fail to consider how much time it took to get the appointment, prepare for the appointment, and all the resources that go into selling the new client.

So many times, these two mistakes are magnified because we assume we will always have good months, seasons, and years. But what happens when economies change, clients leave, and competition closes in? We have to have reserves, be prepared, and we need to live within our means.

Discover, update, and constantly rediscover your hourly, daily, weekly and monthly rates of income so that you know what your real value is. Shop, compare, ask yourself good questions about all purchases, and buy cautiously.

I really wish I had understood this earlier! Fortunately, I learned from my mistakes, and my new businesses have been thriving with my income making a full recovery.

Chapter 42

Advice Streams of Income

When you have good advice and information, there are several business models you may want consider. After all, there is more than one way to monetize your knowledge and experiences.

First, you can start a Mastermind. In a true Mastermind you are generally limited to about twelve people, where one or two typically serve as facilitators to keep things on track and on time. Everyone in a Mastermind should be a pretty equal catalyst in creating ideas and solutions for each other.

Each person will generally get forty-five to sixty minutes over the course of two days to talk about themselves, explain what is really working, and then ask questions about what they need help with. The group then responds with constructive feedback, trade secrets, and service providers.

Next you have Informational Products. This generally consists of information taught through multi-media such as workbooks, audio and video.

New digital methods of creation have made this an easier market to get into. It has also reduced shipping costs and the time it takes to deliver your product to people.

Then you have Group Coaching, which should not be confused with Masterminds. In Group Coaching, one person is the main facilitator and catalyst for the group. This means most people pay and come because of the group coach or catalyst, not necessarily because of the group participants.

Most of the information, exercises, and advice come from the Group Coach. Some interactivity will come from the group, which can be much larger because not everyone needs to get a lot of time to share in this model.

Next is Membership Programs. These are highly desirable because they create more passive residual income, which leads to a more steady income. There is regular monthly content provided in an exclusive setting that is password protected.

There is typically a higher setup cost in creating these, and attrition can be high. Technically, large organizations like AAA and the NRA are membership programs that are making hundreds of millions of dollars.

Subscription programs are very similar to membership programs in the sense that they provide exclusive monthly information. Subscription programs take the shape of newsletters, newspapers, and magazines.

Subscriptions can be both print and digital. Just look at what we are doing with our video print technology and system. This also generates sponsorship and advertiser income, in addition to subscription fees.

You can have a radio or TV show, driven by sponsors or your own wallet. The exposure and credibility can be amazing, but unless you can justify the costs compared to the ad revenue, or can count on high sales from pitching infomercial style, then this option may not make sense.

New developments in satellite technology, cable TV, and XM radio are creating new opportunities all the time for Icon Advisors.

Producing and hosting events can give you a platform and an audience to give, serve, and share with. If done right, it will also provide you the opportunity to sell your products and services.

Events have various models with various factors; they are really their own industry.

If you can keep it simple and build with a free-ticket model, you can generally get something going. But keep in mind that when it's free, people can easily change their mind not to attend on the day of the event.

Certification and licensing programs, if done right, are quite lucrative as well. An Icon can sell his or her system, the training materials, the proven formula for success, and problem solving, and even the rights to use the brand.

I have personally participated, promoted, and leveraged all of these business models at one time or another. All of these streams of income vary in investment and skillsets, but one thing is for sure: The more influential and credible you are, the better the chance you have to create these other advice-driven profit centers.

The bigger the Icon, the bigger the opportunities.

Part IV

Your Icon Evolution

"Success at anything will always come down to this:

Focus and Effort.

And we control both."

~ Dawyne 'The Rock' Johnson

Chapter 43

Change Who You Sell To

It's time to share one of the biggest secrets (actually three of them) that separate those who want to be successful from those who actually do something about it. It's all about knowing when to change and how to evaluate potential change. It looks like this:

1. Change Who You Sell To
2. Change How You Market and Sell
3. Change What You Sell

These are the three key strategies that will make the biggest positive differences in your bottom line.

Change Who You Sell To

For decades, Disney was a powerhouse entertainment company that catered to the family experience by providing the stuff of dreams, imagination, and perfect memories. In 1986, Disney decided it was time to expand its market reach and to sell to a different group of people. Who wasn't already enamored with Disney's theme parks? Business people. Disney created the Disney Institute, a new entity meant to reach businesspeople, and it is still alive and well today. The creative Disney management team recognized an opportunity when they saw one— namely the many company executives who approached them asking for tips on how to train their leaders in the Disney manner.

The company is well known for its loyal and diverse staff, and teaching their recipes for success was just a natural way to expand. The

Disney Institute teaches leadership, creativity, inspiration, and service, to name just a few. Classes are held all over the world and online to boot. This newest arm of the entertainment conglomerate has added tens of millions of dollars in profits to an already outrageously profitable business.

For decades, Mercedes was the brand known for its high-end automobiles and the exclusivity that went along with owning one. Mercedes owners were considered to be in an elite class, and many people bought them as a symbol of status. Extreme performance, safety, and power were all part of the Mercedes image.

When you're already at the top and selling to the world's most affluent people, how can a company expand? In order to sell to another group of people, Mercedes eventually introduced more affordable cars to their top-end lineup. Some were afraid that this would hurt the image of Mercedes as an elite group, but if this has happened, it isn't apparent on the bottom line. There are still plenty of owners who opt for the status symbol of the higher end models, but now they are joined by another class of people who can also afford to enjoy the performance, safety, and power of Mercedes products.

The University of Phoenix could have approached education like every other major school by recruiting young high school graduates, but instead it focused on attracting the working adult. University of Phoenix, otherwise known as the Apollo Group, has earned more than $500 million in revenue per quarter in past years.

The untraditional and under-served target market of adult students has proved very profit able for the Apollo Group. Since the university's success, scores of other major schools have transitioned their marketing efforts to the same demographic that the University of Phoenix had the vision and forethought to target.

Ask yourself these questions in order to identify a new target market:

1. What groups and markets are ready for your products and

services?

2. How can you teach others about your business model and be paid for it?

3. How could you go from local to national to global? Does it make sense to do so right now?

4. How could your partners and affiliates help you reach new markets and demo graphics?

Try these things to find new markets to sell to:

Look at what your competitors are doing to reach new or untapped markets.

Make a list of all the demographic groups you can think of such as women, minorities, home owners, political-party members, etc. Which of these might be interested in your products or services?

Think about and determine how you can create higher-priced versions of your products and services.

Think about and determine how you can create more affordable versions of your products and services.

Chapter 44

Change How You Market and Sell

Netflix began as a fierce little startup back in the days of the VCR, when it was necessary for consumers to walk into a store like Blockbuster and rent a movie to watch at home. Netflix's business plan of simply mailing videos to customers, rather than bearing the overhead expense of a retail store, put them in direct competition with Blockbuster.

Many expected this business model to fail. After all, why wait for a movie to come in the mail when you can simply drive to the corner store and watch what you want tonight?

In modern times, the availability of movies online has completely changed the movie rental industry. Blockbuster, which refused to change its model before it was too late, has gone almost entirely out of business. Netflix executives, however, had the forethought to change how the company marketed and sold movies to their customers. Now, with the days of renting physical movies nearly at an end, Netflix is phasing out its mail service and focusing solely on offering movies, TV shows, documentaries, and music through its online service. Today the company is not only surviving. It is thriving because it changed with the times.

The movie theatre industry, like any other, must stay afloat by finding fresh ways to present and deliver in this age of instant gratification via the Internet. In the past decade or so, the 3D movie has made a comeback.

Many times, you now have an option to see a newly released movie in a regular format or in 3D, but 3D will always costs more. It's the same movie being shown in the same theatre, but now it comes with just another way to market and sell it and for the movie theatre to make more money. The extra cost to make a 3D movie is nowhere near the 20 percent markup in ticket price, so the profit potential is much higher. First, it was just kids' movies, but now even horror films are being made in 3D for higher profits.

Jay Levinson started his Guerrilla Marketing conglomerate with books as the main products, the first being published in 1984. Later, he transformed the company by offering keynote speeches (hearing someone like Jay speak in person is an experience not easily forgotten) and info products, such as an association and Mastermind meetings. It's a lot of the same information, if not exactly the same, just delivered in a different format.

Need some help thinking of new and different ways to market and sell your company's offerings? Answer these questions:

1. How many different ways are you marketing and selling your products and services?
2. What ways are your competitors marketing, selling, and delivering their products and services that you are not?
3. What new media types can you use to promote your business to a fresh target market?

Try the following things to get farther faster with the right changes in the way you market and sell:

1. Share ad space with complementary companies, partners, and affiliates.
2. Look into barter companies where you can trade services for exposure.
3. Determine the ROI on the current marketing media your company relies on; do a feasibility study to determine the best use of your ad budget.
4. Get creative with your packaging. Is it time to update it with

a new, fresh design?

I realize there is no reason to reinvent the wheel, but by packaging the wheel differently, you can make nearly unlimited incremental revenue to add to your bottom line.

Chapter 45

Change What You Market and Sell

Most celebrities make their money from ticket sales to movies and sporting events. When they want bigger profitability, they capitalize on their name to sell fragrances, clothing, and even open their own restaurants.

Martha Stewart has a line of housewares with several different retailers; Tim McGraw has his own cologne; Cindy Crawford has her own furniture collection; George Foreman has his grill; Cindy Crawford has her makeup line; and Mark Wahlberg's family uses his name to sell "Wahlburgers."

Why stick to keynote speeches and book revenue when a famous guru can get paid solely for his advice? Many successful speakers and authors offer coaching and consulting as an adjunct to their main business.

Tony Robbins, Mark Victor Hansen, Bill Clinton, Deepak Chopra and T. Harv Eker are just a few. Tony will make more money coaching and consulting than he will with his books and keynotes, but he couldn't have one without the other, or at least not on the same level.

Some decades ago, gas stations stopped offering full-service pumps and instead opted to selling things other than gas in order to earn incremental revenue that quickly added to the bottom line. In addition to their basic operations, most stations added racks of snack foods and coolers full of soda.

This evolved to full convenience markets, and most now house mini versions of your favorite fast food restaurants. Once, small corner stations with a couple of pumps and perhaps a service bay were common; today those corner gas stations are now 20,000 square-foot-plus buildings with several lanes of pumps and the clean feel of a mall inside.

Amway, once known as the most popular multi-level marketing business in the U.S. during the 1960s, has had to change what it sells in order to keep up with the modern age. Rather than stock a full inventory of grocery and household products in their garages, Amway distributors now use the drop-ship system and focus on eco-friendly items that appeal to a higher-income demographic. Amway's Naturelife brand is not only more popular than other products with today's consumer; it also commands a higher price point.

Has your business changed with the times? The products and services you offer might be overdue for a revamp. Think of answers to these questions to start considering ways you can change what you sell:

1. Find five other examples on your own to experience this belief for yourself.
2. What complementary products can you offer in addition to your proven sales leaders?
3. What sponsors could use your endorsement or access to your list?
4. What other industries do you share a client base with?

Try these things to learn what else you can sell

1. Explore ways to make products out of your industry knowledge or specialized training.
2. Research what your competition offers beyond their "bread and butter" products or services.
3. Search for affiliates who already have "done for you" information products ready to sell to your target market.
4. Research what other products and services consumers use with yours.

Chapter 46

Dreaming is Good, but Doing is Better

Sometimes I think, "I hate dreamers." But then I remember my mom taught me not to hate. Other times I want to say, "Dreamers annoy me." But then I realize that isn't necessarily true either. Here is the best way to explain myself:

"Dreaming is Good, but Doing is Better."

I'll take a small-time doer over a big-time dreamer any old day. The billion dollar Nike motto is "Just Do It"—not "Just Dream It." There is a reason for that.

The key to more doing is to really reverse engineer your final destination. Discover where you want to be, and then work backward. Once you know the path, you can break things down into baby steps. Here are some easy questions that can lead you to super simple steps.

1. What do you really want?
2. We all want money as a means to an end, but what is that end?
3. We all want more time, but what do you want to do with that time?
4. What kind of businesses and day-to-day activities do you like?

Most people can run lots of different kinds of businesses as long as they get to spend time working on things they enjoy and make the most money in the least amount of time. In theory, I could be happy running a gym, a restaurant, or even a private school for entrepreneur-minded kids. As long as I am creating, marketing, transforming, selling, and ultimately providing amazing results and magical experiences, I am happy.

BEWARE: Although you can do lots of different things as a sales person or entrepreneur, don't be that ADHD person who chases every shiny object. Once you pick a business, stick to it for a set time!

Choose a time frame like three months, six months, or even a year, and then really work that business. If you can't commit to that, then you shouldn't even start. The benefit of doing this is to ensure you don't give up in the heat of the moment during a bad day or a bad month. Taking action in a consistent, on-purpose way is very powerful. Who knows where I would be if I just quit every time I hit a pothole.

Once you know what you want and have set a time frame for making it work, tell someone about your plan of action so they can help hold you accountable. An accountability partner is para mount. I ignored the details and tried to do too much for a long time. It was my wife who became my accountability partner—whether I liked it or not. Jill asked me the tough questions. She asked me about the details and the numbers. Although it was annoying at times, it made me commit to my planned actions, and it gave me someone to answer to.

Last but not least: do whatever it takes to execute the actions necessary to be successful. Be bold, work hard, and, just short of breaking the law, do whatever it takes!

In the last fifteen years of sales and owning my own businesses, I have had two different night jobs. One time I unloaded 53-foot-long trucks for FedEx making $10 an hour. Even though it was at night, it was in Phoenix during the summer. Sometimes it was still close to 100 degrees, and the inside of those trucks were not any cooler. I went to work all day, had dinner with the family, took a nap, and then unloaded trucks from 10PM to 2AM.

We did whatever it took to keep going—to keep taking action. I'd love to say I never gave up, but there were some bad days. And then a new day would come, and I would start again…taking action! Maybe now you can see why my tolerance for dreamers who never do is so thin.

Don't just dream! DO!

Do what it takes to become more influential, credible, and to get more exposure so that you can Crack the Icon Code and monetize your knowledge and experiences.

"LAW OF ATTRACTION
WITHOUT *ACTION*
IS JUST A FRACTION"
- DAVID T. FAGAN

Chapter 47

Icon or Idiot

After spending all of these chapters telling you what Icons are and what Icon Advisors do, I want to tell you what they are not and what they don't do. There really is a fine line that can't be crossed.

In the pursuit of associations with successful people, testimonials, endorsements, awards, degrees, media attention, and social proof in general an Icon can actually alienate people if he or she self-promotes too much or too hard.

That's one of the reasons why Icons want third-party promoting— so that they aren't seen as conceited people constantly bragging about all their accomplishments. Any self-promoting must come from a place of just trying to earn someone's business and applying for a job.

I've known several people including a Realtor in Arizona who said, "I'm not bragging; I'm applying for a job. I want to be your Realtor." He does quite well with that line, and I have since shared it.

Part of being an Icon Advisor is what I call "making your presence felt," meaning you should stand out to people in a good way. This can include how you dress, your accessories, what you drive, where you live, and how you communicate, verbally and with your body language.

On the other hand, it's possible to over dress, over accessorize, and over buy, which will just be perceived as flaunting your money. It is very polarizing and is a huge turn off.

As I've already pointed out, it is even more important that you do not sink yourself into huge amounts of debt just to look good. Quite simply, this is wrong and I do not support it in any way. I made some of these mistakes in my earlier years, and I paid dearly for them.

One of the hardest things you will ever do is to figure out how to build and balance your social proof without going over the top and alienating the people around you.

One way to keep this balance is to be vulnerable and share your mistakes and failures as much as your successes.

Another way to strike a balance is to realize that the more people and organizations celebrate you, the less you should promote yourself. In the beginning, you may promote yourself more, but as your social proof progresses, the more you should limit your self-promotions. Other than that, you should be cool. Put a little ICE in your veins, become an Icon in your industry, and leverage the systems in this book to monetize your knowledge and experiences.

If I mention the name Kim Kardashian what comes to mind. Is she an icon or an idiot? Some might say she is just on television because she is beautiful but there are a lot of beautiful women in the world. Some might say she is just got on television because she is rich but there are a lot of rich women out there too. More than you might realize.

Some might say it's just a fad but for years she has been building her empire. Some might say it's not really her and that she just has successful people all around her but so does the rest of her family she seems to do the best by far. Plus, doesn't she deserve some credit for having good people around her?

You can still dislike her or even hate her but can you also learn something from her?

In Forbes 2015 list of top paid celebrities Kim Kardashian beat out quite a few actresses including Jennifer Lawrence. Think about that. Jennifer for the last few previous years has been nominated and won multiple awards for acting plus she is a part of one of the top selling movie franchises of all time the Hunger Games. Yet Kim, a reality tv star, made tens of millions of dollars and beat out Jennifer on the list of top paid celebrities.

This is just further proof that visibility can equal credibility. And by the way, I'm not saying it should be that way I am just saying it is that way. That is the rule that is proven with only a few exceptions.

So will she go down in history as an icon or as an idiot?

Donald Trump, Judge Judy, Tony Hawk and Howard Stern all know how to play the game. They are icons in their industry aren't they?

The average judge in the US make 100k a year. Judge Judy made about 40 million in 2015. The average professional skateboarder makes tens of thousands of dollars a year. Tony Hawk is worth 2 billion!

So icons or idiots? It's a tough call on some of these people we see paraded through the media but I love the simple two option method. Bill O'reilly has patriot or pinhead as a segment on his show. Rotten Tomatoes only allows the rating of fresh or rotten for users and critics alike.

I even suppose icons can become idiots and idiots can become icons but to know the line is important. To recognize the line and to be able to learn from people is even better. A lot of money can be made for those that create an icon status and learn how to monetize it.

I don't judge icons based on whether or not I agree with their politics, personal opinions or whether or not I even like them personally. I judge them on their ability to counter balance their talents, beliefs, and brand all while maintaining a strong base of fans. This is not easy and I have a lot of respect for people who can make a lot of money doing what they love.

I actually just saw the world's fastest marathon juggler do a commercial for Marriott! Crazy what successes can be monetized.

The success, the talent, and the results must come first, the brand second and the big money last. Remember, Tiger Woods, David Beckham, Rush Limbaugh, Ellen Degeneres, Lebron James and all the other icons make most of their money through endorsements because of their brand. When their brand hurts sponsors leave.

Just look at Kobe Bryant, Paula Deen, Tiger Woods, and Charlie Sheen. There is nothing wrong with strategic controversy but famous is better than infamous almost every time. You can only alienate so many people before it hurts the bank account in a way that you may never fully recover from.

The idiots to me are the ones who change their minds too much, listen to the wrong people, the ones who don't know who they are, what they stand for or how show up in this world. I especially lose a lot of respect for the ones who forget who made them successful in the first place. I'm a big believer that we need to vote with our wallets.

We can learn from the everyday icons we see in the media. They have entourages, they get nominated and win awards, they monetize their brands with various product lines, they have social media pages, websites, write books, appear on TV and in the movies even if it's just a cameo, they get good pictures, they have unique perspectives, they have passion, they create businesses, they form joint ventures, they have publicists, agents and support staff, and these icons all have fans!

You want to impress someone make your presence felt sometime. You want the respect of die-hard fans stay relevant and be consistent.

Just keep asking yourself icon or idiot.

So don't forget to keep learning, growing, and experiencing. In most of this book, we examined how to create a profitable Icon status based on your current knowledge and experiences, but you need to keep reading, studying, and having a mentor who will guide you.

This Icon Code needs to be continually cracked, and new mysteries will need to be solved all the time. The pursuit of social proof can never stop in order for you to "stay relevant." It's a life long journey that never has any final destination rather just a series of successful summits along the way.

Give, Serve, and Share strategically to have the most fans. Document all of your successes, and employ an army of fans to bring you more business. Advice based on your knowledge and experiences with a profitable process in place that leverages automation is fundamental in cracking the code. Remember, it's being both an Icon and an Advisor that ultimately cracks the Icon Code. From there, it's only up to your direct discipline of implementing a pipeline with a purpose that will allow you to unlock all the wealth that an Icon Advisor truly deserves.

Be Heard, Be Seen, Get Paid!

David T. Fagan

THE DAVID T. FAGAN MANTRA

WHY DO I SUCCEED?

I SUCCEED BECAUSE I AM WILLING TO DO
THE THINGS THAT OTHERS ARE NOT.
I WILL FIGHT AGAINST THE ODDS AND I WILL
SACRIFICE. AFTER ALL, I HAVE LEARNED TO
LOVE PEOPLE UNDERESTIMATING ME.

I SUCCEED BECAUSE I AM NOT SHACKLED
BY FEAR, INSECURITY OR DOUBT.
YES, I FEEL THESE EMOTIONS TOO BUT THEN
I STARE THEM DOWN, DRINK THEM IN
AND THEN SWALLOW THEM AWAY
TO THE BLACKNESS OF OBLIVION.

I SUCCEED BECAUSE I HAVE AN
UNWAVERING CONVICTION THAT MY LIFE
HAS MEANING AND THAT I AM A FORCE
TO BE RECKONED WITH. I PRACTICE AND
PREPARE TO MEET MY OPPORTUNITIES
WITH FIERCE EXECUTION.

IF I FALL, I WILL GET UP. IF I AM
BEATEN, I WILL RETURN. I WILL NEVER
STOP GETTING BETTER, NEVER.

THIS IS WHY I SUCCEED.

WWW.DAVIDTFAGAN.COM   WWW.INVISIBLETOINVINCIBLEBOOK.COM

My mantra can become your mantra.

Icon Reading List

Here are the other Top 10 books that every Icon Advisor (anyone in the Advice Business) should read, in no particular order:

1. *Guerrilla Marketing* by Jay Conrad Levinson
2. *It's Not Over Until You Win* by Les Brown
3. *Guerrilla PR* by Michael Levine
4. *The Art of Significance* by Dan Clark
5. *How to Win Friends and Influence People* by Dale Carnegie
6. *Winning with People* by John C. Maxwell
7. *48 Laws of Power* by Robert Greene
8. *Conquer the Chaos* by Clate Mask and Scott Martineau
9. *High Trust Selling* by Todd Duncan
10. *The Fred Factor* by Mark Sanborn

Dictionary

Agent – representative that sells your bool to publishers for a percentage; also called literary or book agents

Brand – the sum total of all the experiences people have had with any person, place or thing (including products and organizations).

Designer – person dealing mostly with the graphics, images, and overall visual appeal; may also be the individual that designs the inside and outside of a book

Emotional Trigger – words and images that evoke the feeling you want a person or group to experience

Fulfillment – the portion of the business transaction where client momentum is created, expectations are set, and credits are placed in the relationship bank; also where project deliverables are created and given to client

Icon – a person who is really successful and admire; a person who has fans

Law of Exaggeration – the art of overstating or exaggerating to draw attention to your points

Law of Multiplication – marketing and selling one message multiple ways, multiple times, to multiple people

Moniker – another name that references who you are, for business people and celebrities, it can be a sophisticated or memorable nick name

Pipeline – system for tracking how many people you need to work with in the beginning in order to meet your financial goals

Programmer – person that writes code typically from scratch to create a new website or to tweak an existing web theme in order to maximize it

Prospects – people that have been exposed to you and your organization

Referral Partner – people you build a relationship with that will promote and recommend you to people they know

Segment – a soundbite that is expanded into a two- to three-minute piece; often includes an image that helps people focus more on how you want them to feel

Soundbite – a short phrase or sentence that captures the essence of what the speaker was trying to say, and is used to summarize information

Suspects – people that opt in to your database, connect with you through Social Media, and are referred to you in some way

About the Author

David Teancum Fagan was born in 1976, in the Fort Hood Army Hospital in Killeen, Texas, where his father Vernon Fagan Jr. was stationed. David is the oldest of six kids, with five younger sisters. Although David's family made a few significant moves when he was growing up, including a short time being stationed in what was once West Germany, David mostly grew up in various small towns in Oregon.

David left high school in the fall of his 11th grade year, opting for a GED and eventually moving out on his own when he was 17. He later went to some college classes at the University of Phoenix, paid for or reimbursed by his employer at the time, Wells Fargo Bank. Although he didn't graduate from Harvard, he also took courses there as part of a program for CEOs. David firmly believes in customizing an education and that traditional schooling isn't for everyone.

THE TWO MOST IMPORTANT DAYS IN YOUR LIFE ARE THE DAY YOU ARE **BORN**, AND THE DAY YOU FIND OUT **WHY**.

– MARK TWAIN

David married Jill Packard in the late 1990s, and they have nine children but are raising eight due to one full-term baby passing away during birth in January 2006. Jill has been pregnant nine times for nine months each, or about seven full years of the entire 17 years they've been together.

When David and Jill met, David had just passed the tests necessary to become an officer for the Phoenix Police Department. During the slow hiring process, David took a job at a bank and ended up being there for almost five years.

Since 1994, David has almost always been involved in sales and marketing. Since 2002, he has almost always worked for himself. His jobs and businesses mostly involved banking and real estate until about 2007, when he reinvented himself in the world of business development, marketing, and publicity helping others grow their businesses.

David believes he really found himself, started his family, and developed his talents while living in Arizona for roughly twelve years. Other than a lifestyle experiment of living in the Northwest on a 10-acre farm, he has most recently lived in Southern California.

Currently David and his family live in San Juan Capistrano, California six miles from Dana Point Harbor, where he keeps his sailboat.

Today, he is best known as a speaker, author, and entrepreneur as the Icon Builder with his marketing and PR company based out of Beverly Hills, CA. He is the former CEO of Guerrilla Marketing, which sold over 23 million books in 62 languages all over the world. He's also the former owner of LCO Communications, which has represented 58 Academy Award Winners, 34 Grammy Winners, and 43 New York Times bestsellers.

David owns Icon Builder Media, is a guest lecturer at UCLA, and has been recently featured in *Fox & Friends, The Washington Post, Forbes, The Today Show, Fox's the Five, Neil Cavuto, The Doctors Show, ABC's 20/20, Investor's Business Daily, Yahoo! News, The Wrap*, and the *Los Angeles Business Journal,* and many more media outlets.

An international speaker in places as far away as Bangladesh and Australia, he has shared the stage with Former Secretary of Defense Dr. Bob Gates, Mark Victor Hansen, Dan Kennedy, Harry Dent, and John Assaraf to name a few.

David loves to sail, play basketball, coach his kids, and bicycle.

David also has a passion for training Teen Entrepreneurs and for a movement he calls Guerrilla Parenting, which is best represented in his bestselling book, *Guerrilla Parenting: How to Raise an Entrepreneur,* released in April 2015.